self-care for winter

self-care for winter

seven steps to thriving
in the colder months

SUZY READING

ASTER*

ASTER

For Charlotte and Teddy, may you thrive wherever you are in the world

First published in Great Britain in 2024 by Aster, an imprint of Octopus Publishing Group Ltd Carmelite House 50 Victoria Embankment London EC4Y 0DZ www.octopusbooks.co.uk

An Hachette UK Company www.hachette.co.uk

The authorized representative in the EEA is Hachette Ireland, 8 Castlecourt Centre, Dublin 15, D15 XTP3, Ireland (email: info@hbgi.ie)

Text copyright © Suzy Reading 2024 Illustrations copyright © Rosanna Tasker 2024 Design and layout copyright © Octopus Publishing Group 2024

Distributed in the US by Hachette Book Group 1290 Avenue of the Americas 4th and 5th Floors, New York, NY 10104

Distributed in Canada by Canadian Manda Group, 664 Annette St. Toronto, Ontario, Canada M6S 2C8

Suzy Reading has asserted her right under the Copyright, Designs and Patents Act 1988 to be identified as the author of this work.

ISBN 978-1-78325-635-8

A CIP catalogue record for this book is available from the British Library.

Printed and bound in Poland

10 9 8 7 6 5 4 3

Commissioning editor: Jessica Lacey
Senior developmental editor: Pauline Bache
Art director: Yasia Williams
Illustrator: Rosanna Tasker
Production managers: Nic Jones and Lucy Carter

All reasonable care has been taken in the preparation of this book but the information it contains is not intended to take the place treatment by a qualified medical practitioner.

Before making any changes in your health regime, always consult a doctor. While all the therapies detailed in this book are completely safe if done correctly, you must seek professional advice if you are in any doubt about any medical condition. Any application of the ideas and information contained in this book is at the reader's sole discretion and risk.

Contents

Introduction

The leaves in all their magnificent golden hues have fallen, the evenings are drawing in and we've crossed the threshold into the deep, dark winter months. There are milky pink mornings, crisp fresh air that sharpens your focus, the nodding encouragement of snowdrops promising the rebirth of spring, and a silence and stillness that feels calming to the senses. Do you feel it too? The genuine urge to cocoon, a growing need for rest, a deep desire to seek comfort? For some people, winter is a treasured time of year – one that is happily embraced – but for many others it is a tough season to weather, and for good reason.

As a psychologist, my job involves supporting people through stress, loss and change – often across prolonged periods of time and seasons. Many people find winter a genuinely challenging time of year, with deep fatigue and diminished productivity, and these feelings are often met with harsh self-criticism for not being able to "push through". If you feel this too, you're in excellent company; some two million people report being affected by winter in the UK alone[1]. Perhaps you've noticed an increased need for sleep, cravings for comfort food, low energy, the dreaded blues? Analysis of social media posts shows a peak of sadness in the winter[2]. And it's not just our mood and energy levels that are impacted: winter can make it hard to pitch up, focus, learn and remember, too[3]. Research has shown that the cognitive performance of people living with Alzheimer's disease varies with the seasons, with symptoms worse in winter[4], but it's not only clinical populations that are affected – no one is immune.

However, observe the ways the plant and animal kingdoms respond to the environmental cues of winter. Bears hibernate, geese migrate, the arctic fox changes her coat and trees conserve moisture by shedding their leaves. So why do we humans expect ourselves to be unaffected? As the days become shorter and the cold descends, hibernation mode is very real. We feel the invitation to slow down, retreat and take stock. It's not just you.

The truth is that modern life makes it hard to listen to this call to pause, recalibrate and commit to a more compassionate pace, and I think it is fair to say from the outset that life does feel harder in the winter. It can feel lonely and desolate. No one wants to be "left out in the cold". In winter, when the conditions are more challenging, our self-care should get bumped up our list of priorities, but let's acknowledge how tricky this can be when energy is running low. It takes a little more effort to get the same rejuvenation from Nature. It takes genuine planning and preparation to keep ourselves nourished, hydrated, moving and connected. Without us being intentional and proactive, winter can be seriously depleting, weighing heavily on us. So we know it hurts, but how can we protect ourselves?

I want to uplift and inspire you in this book with ways that will encourage you to savour winter: to embrace the cosy comfort, the pleasure of retreating together and, on occasion, getting out into the natural delights that are unique to this season. I hope this reminder brings you comfort: you're not lazy or weak, it's just winter! But, at the same time, I will show you how to be respectful of the challenges winter brings. This book will guide you in formulating your own self-care plan to navigate this season. It's more than just about mindset, it's an approach that encompasses our outlook, develops core skills and galvanizes us to take action.

I will introduce you to the three Cs: **Curiosity, Compassion** and **Care**. These three themes are woven throughout the book through invitations to check in and notice what feels resonant and relevant to you. They are reminders to be gentle and realistic in your observations and action planning and, at the end of each step, you'll find reflective prompts to help you become crystal clear on your commitments to yourself.

- **Curiosity** refers to openness to experiences, new ways of thinking, refining our ability to notice not only natural beauty available to us in winter but to also recognize our own human needs.

- **Compassion** refers to extending a quality of gentleness and tenderness towards ourselves. At the heart of compassion lies the permission to feel as we do and to temper our pace and expectations of ourselves in response.

- **Care** is where the action comes in. It's not enough just to notice our needs, to be accepting of ourselves as we are – we must also reach out for the nourishment or support that will help us cope in winter, whether this is something we can extend to ourselves or some form of care we need to request from others.

I will show you how to use curiosity, compassion and care to build your winter self-care plan. Using the three Cs, we're going to honour the natural impulses that come with this season, while striking a healthy balance to meet the real and present demands of your life. In following your natural desire to seek comfort, I'm going to share soothing practices that will help you in the moment without making tomorrow harder. You can think of this self-care plan as a scaffolding of healthy habits, both giving shape to your day and providing you with the energy you need to meet the pressures of life.

As you heed the call to slow down, I'm going to teach you concrete ways to effectively alter your pace. In recognizing your increased need for rest and sleep, together we will break through the barrier of guilt and commit to tangible actions that will replenish you. You might feel like hibernating, but I'm going to share movement practices with you that will help you feel alive even when energy and motivation is at zero. Even when the great outdoors doesn't appeal in the slightest, I'm going to show you how to get your daily dose of Nature Therapy. When you feel the desire to socially retreat, I will show you how to stay connected. If you notice the desire to reflect, I'll guide you through simple prompts that will uplift you while avoiding the potential overwhelm that can come from turning inwards without direction.

Thriving

While we stay anchored in the reality of the winter months, let's not set our sights on just weathering them. Let's aim for something far more life-giving. I'd love to remove the winter dread and replace it with hopeful anticipation. Winter dread trains our eyes to see all the things we don't enjoy, whereas hopeful anticipation taps into that sense of curiosity about what's possible. I hope that in sharing the gifts, purpose and meaning exclusive to winter, you might be on the lookout for them and when our minds are open, we are far more likely to receive them.

Research supports this approach: psychologist Kari Leibowitz spent a year living 350km (more than 200 miles) north of the Arctic Circle in Tromsø, Norway, studying how people coped with such extreme environmental conditions. In this place, so far north that the sun doesn't even rise for two months of the year, Leibowitz investigated how people were able to not only survive but thrive in these harsh conditions. She discovered that many Norwegians genuinely love winter and that this mindset was positively associated with well-being, life satisfaction and personal growth[5].

Leibowitz found that the locals who saw it as an opportunity to do the things they loved, such as skiing, relishing cosiness indoors and having a chance to see the mesmerising northern lights, tended to be happier overall. It's worth noting that while locals enjoyed the chance to hunker down, they still made the commitment to regular movement. And while I know the winter wonderland there can seem very different to the dull and sometimes lifeless grey of urban winter scenes, there is still a leaf we can take from the Norwegians' books – we can get curious about the opportunities that are present and we can savour the joys unique to winter.

This is not about glossing over the challenges and just thinking positive, it's about staying grounded in what we can do and maximizing available pleasure.

As an Australian living in the UK, I am blessed with the childlike curiosity of an "out-of-towner", giving me fresh eyes to the pleasures inherent to the winter months in the Northern Hemisphere. I've lost count of the times locals marvel when they learn my country of origin, leaving them gobsmacked that I would actively choose this climate over the perpetually summery climes of my native home. But the truth is that many of my peak life moments from nearly two decades of living in the UK are wintry ones. The dark and cold makes sleep deeper, more delicious and easier to come by. As much as I relish the outward-facing nature of summer, basking like a lizard where possible and drinking in lingering summer evenings, I also enjoy the feeling of turning inwards that is available to us in winter. A different pace. A different purpose. A different natural beauty.

One of my most vivid early memories was seeing my first snowfall as a child when visiting the UK. This was my first (and so far) only "white Christmas", but I finally understood "Season's Greetings" cards with the frosty white landscapes. The way the streetlamps caught the flakes as they fell; the silence created by the blanket covering every nook and cranny; the promise of tomorrow's blank canvas. I loved waking to the plethora of pawprints in the snow from unknown nocturnal creatures – the wonderful reminder that winter isn't all about death and decay, she is still teeming with life.

Now that I'm a local to the Northern Hemisphere, and it's not new anymore, I enjoy the satisfaction of stowing away the summer hats and digging out the winter woollies in preparation for a world that feels fresh and new, as if the cold has given everything a deep clean. I love how the shroud of white snow transforms familiar everyday scenes into something magical, something unrecognizable. The excitement remains palpable – it's always a complete disruption to normal life where we indulge in all the wintry delights.

The snow reminds us of Nature's awe-inspiring power: that few things can bring life to a grinding halt. When we see the plume of our breath or hear the sound of snow crunching underfoot, it is a precious opportunity to savour the sensory experiences exclusive to winter. It's a chance to zoom in and see the power of Nature's beauty in full force – whether that's the intricate fractal patterns of snowflakes or frost-encrusted cars glinting like diamonds in the morning light. Winter turns even the most humdrum landscape into exquisite works of art.

In the vast space between the snow days, there is a distinct beauty to the silhouette of bare branches against the stark sky, revealing the inhabitants of the trees formerly obscured by lush foliage. This gives the conifers their turn to shine. Misty rain drops gathering on Nature's naked limbs are her string of pearls, and frozen spiderwebs, her tinsel. We see bright red berries adorning the hedgerow and the eruption of snowdrops, crocuses and primrose – the Earth isn't dead, she's just sleeping.

On occasion, the winter skyscapes themselves are breathtaking with light shows unique to this time of year. Granted, there might be days where it feels like we've not seen the sun at all, but when she appears on clear days, it's a light like no other time of year – glowing and ethereal. After a particularly bleak stretch, I can remember going for a walk along the canal in an attempt to blow away the mental cobwebs. The hedge to my side cast a shadow from my neck down but as the sun emerged from behind the clouds, I could feel the light bathe the back of my head like two cupped hands, all the sweeter for its prior absence. An experience of maybe 30 seconds, but one that has stayed with me for years. I've since learned there is a word for this experience: apricity, meaning the warmth of the winter sun, and my eyes have become fine-tuned to seek it.

Now for the flipside.

In addition to these peak life moments, winter is the cold and flu season and for parents of school-age kids or public transport commuters, it's not unusual for at least one person in your nest to be afflicted for months on end. There is the constant battle with winter condensation, arguments about central heating and worries about the cost of it all. Tempers are short and it's hard rising in the darkness, then returning home in the darkness. There are miserable school runs in the mud and rain, plus all the bribing, begging and cajoling to get bodies out of the door, even when we're going out to do something joyful. The piling on of all the layers and then the washing and drying of soggy layers upon return. The cold manifests in numb fingers, groaning arthritic joints, chilblained toes, chapped lips, reptile-like cracked hands.

The hum of low-grade anxiety continues for months on end due to the uncertainty of weather and travel conditions affecting our ability to honour the commitments we've made, and the mourning of cancelled treasured plans. Even without the snow and ice, driving conditions in poor light can feel treacherous and make the most confident drivers think twice about unnecessary excursions, which for many people can feel isolating.

These are no small things. Winter makes us work hard not only for our joy, but just to get out of our home. There are windscreens to be de-iced, engines to warm, driveways to clear. It demands more of us to just do the basics, let alone the things that are nice to do. The conditions are aversive, the cold hurts and it is depleting. But, from time to time, it is also sublimely beautiful, arguably more glorious than pleasure that has come easily. We just need supportive practices to sustain us and help us eke out winter joy.

The opportunity

The dark deepens our appreciation of light, the cold hones our gratitude for warmth and the variation gives rhythm and pulse to life. The change in the seasons punctuates time, giving shape to the year and these external markers help to denote the passing of time, helping us pace ourselves. It reminds us that there is a natural expansion and contraction present in our environment and this is mirrored within us too. Life isn't linear and our progress and growth needn't be linear either. We are embedded in a cycle of change and our own inner worlds are constantly in a process of becoming, growing, shedding, renewing, coming our own, before beginning again.

It's a metaphor for times of change in our lives, too. Winter has gently guided me through my own life transformations of international relocations, becoming a mother and losing my father. Winter reminds me that these chapters won't last forever and that it's ok to have fallow time – time to fall apart and make space for a fresh new expression of self, having faith that a new identity will emerge. There is time for the bud, time for the bloom, time for decay and every season has its value, its beauty, its place.

Mother Nature has always brought me deep comfort in challenging times and winter is an essential part of that understanding. She not only shows us that it's ok to honour our boundaries and pace ourselves, but Nature shows us how to do it, too. She demonstrates skilful interdependence – how we get through the good times and the bad times by relying on each other. But even here she shows nuance: we don't have to pitch up in all our glory all the time, sometimes our bare presence is more than enough.

She models that the support we offer each other can flex through the seasons and that we don't have to give to our depletion. How we attend to the needs of others when life squeezes us can look different to what we give of ourselves when we're in a place of abundance. Trees don't yield fruit or nuts all year, but they still provide protection in the winter and nourishment via their bark. She shows us that we can still be kind, caring people while honouring our boundaries and preserving our energy and peace.

The long nights of winter give the moon her opportunity to take centre stage too, with her own personal message to all who witness her. Just as the moon goes through phases, so do we. Sometimes we are bright and full, other times, nothing but a sliver – regardless of incarnation, we are always whole, complete and more than enough.

It's not just about fine-tuning our senses to seek out the season's beauty and "thinking positively" about winter, we need a host of tangible supportive practices to help us tweak our pace and maintain our commitments to healthy habits. As a chartered psychologist, I can provide you with the mental health-boosting tools. And as a yoga teacher and personal trainer, I have all the movement, breath and meditative techniques to offer you too.

This is your multimodality toolkit to maximize winter joy – I can't wait to share it with you.

REFLECTION TIME ON WINTER

*Before we begin on our nourishing action planning,
pause for some reflection time of your own.*

~

*How does winter impact on your health and well-being?
What do you notice?*

~

How do you feel about winter and its effects on you?

~

What do you enjoy?

~

What do you find personally challenging?

What is winter self-care?

Let's start with defining self-care. Self-care is how we nourish ourselves to promote, protect or restore our mental, emotional and physical health. The purpose of self-care is to help us cope in times of challenge or high emotion, to help us heal following these chapters of life and to give us a buffer against the next curveball.

Our commitment to nourishing ourselves also helps us access the qualities that we hold dear as human beings and enhances the health of our relationships – when we're well nourished, it's easier to be calm, patient and present. Think of your self-care as the gift that keeps on giving. I hope this helps to dial down any guilt you might feel about prioritizing your health. You still might be feeling like there isn't the time, energy or funds for the self-care you'd like to be doing but, rest assured, I have you covered with the practices in this book!

I have created this book to be your winter well-being companion, an annual guide to bring you home to yourself, to help you develop your own personalized care plan responsive to current life events. The kind of self-care we might engage in when life is smooth can look very different to the time, energy and freedom we have at our disposal in more turbulent periods of our lives – and it's more than ok for our self-care to evolve with the seasons of our life, as well as the seasons of Nature.

I hope the practices in this book will help you find something resonant, accessible and effective during the winter months, respectful of what's unfolding in the personal chapter of your life. Perhaps this is something you can enjoy coming back to, year after year, to determine the course of action to support you through this winter season and into the rebirth of spring.

Every year, we encounter new events, different demands, unique challenges and gifts — I hope you enjoy choosing your own interpretation of self-care to nourish you now knowing that each year it might look entirely different.

And lastly, an essential note on the scope of self-care. While I advocate for all sorts of habits to look after our health and well-being, I am not saying that any human being should be shouldering their burden on their own. Every human being needs love, support and hands-on care from other people. We need to be caring towards ourselves and we also need to be cared for. I hope the practices in this book can be a powerful addition to sound social support.

REFLECTION TIME ON SELF-CARE

How do you feel about the term "self-care"? If it's not a phrase that appeals to you, feel free to think of it as health care, nourishment, energy management or your well-being boosters. Choose whatever resonates and motivates you.

∼

What are your barriers to engaging in the kind of nourishment you'd prefer – is it time, energy, space, freedom, expense or does guilt interfere? Spend some time thinking about ways to overcome these barriers. If you're not sure, don't worry, as you journey through this book, you will learn a whole host of time and energy-efficient practices that don't cost a penny. In my experience, guilt is the most tenacious barrier. At the heart of self-care is our health and without our health what do we have? What does your health allow you to do or be? What important things do you sacrifice when you are feeling depleted?

∼

Write down three reasons why it's not just ok but necessary for you to take care of yourself.

The science of how winter affects our minds & bodies

Cold temperatures and fewer daylight hours can have a profound impact on how we think, feel and behave. We're all familiar with seasonal affective disorder (SAD), but you don't have to be diagnosed with SAD to experience the same symptoms to some extent. Many of the SAD symptoms can be likened to the energy-conserving behaviour that we see exhibited by hibernating animals. The effects that wintry conditions have on our well-being suggests that many people struggle and that a diagnosis of SAD represents only the extreme end of difficulties[6].

The signs of SAD include persistent feelings of sadness, anxiety or emptiness, depressed mood for most of the day, loss of pleasure or interest in activities that are usually enjoyable, lethargy and lack of energy, heavy limbs, decreased libido, feeling irritable, agitated or restless, a sense of hopelessness, helplessness, despair, guilt, worthlessness, difficulty concentrating and remembering, impaired decision-making capacity, social withdrawal, persistent physical aches, pains and digestive complaints, sleeping for longer and finding it harder to wake up in the mornings, cravings for energy-dense food and weight gain[7].

We all feel a touch of these things at times, but for sufferers of SAD it can feel impossible to meet the usual demands of life. If you're concerned that you might be experiencing SAD, seek support from your GP; support is vital and effective interventions are available.

There are a range of treatment options and you and your GP can talk about what combination feels most resonant to you. These include: light therapy (a special light box to simulate exposure to daylight); talking therapies such as counselling or cognitive behaviour therapy; antidepressant medication; and lifestyle tweaks to manage your energy, mood and stress. The remaining steps will help you integrate these healthy habits into everyday life.

While researchers are still establishing the exact causes of seasonal affective disorder, it is commonly accepted to be linked with the reduced sunlight during winter days and these are the theorized underlying mechanisms and contributing factors:

1. Changes to our body clock

Our body clock shifts in response to changing availability of light. Our bodies use sunlight to time internal functions such as when you wake and when you feel sleepy. Lower light levels in winter can disrupt these circadian rhythms, making it harder to meet the usual demands of your day. In times gone by, our daily rhythms would have shifted with the seasonal changes, but with the advent of artificial light and heating, and the pressures of modern life, we are less inclined to alter our pace. However, being out of kilter with our natural rhythms can be discombobulating and depleting.

Scientists studying a hunter-gatherer community in Argentina found that those without access to artificial light in winter slept for 56 extra minutes than those who had access to electricity[8]. Expecting ourselves to be able to carry on in winter with the same hours of alertness and productivity is a recipe for stress and frustration, but the reality is many people don't have the freedom to alter their wake time to allow for this extra seasonal requirement for sleep.

2. Changes to the production of serotonin
Serotonin is one of the brain chemicals that contributes to feelings of happiness. Sunlight helps to regulate serotonin so in winter when there is less sunlight, serotonin levels can fall, leading to depression.

3. Vitamin D deficiency
Serotonin levels are also affected by vitamin D, which is absorbed through the skin when exposed to sunlight. Without adequate access to sunlight, vitamin D levels drop, affecting serotonin levels and thereby diminishing our mood.

4. Melatonin boost
Melatonin is a hormone that plays a role in managing our sleep-wake cycle. The lack of sunlight is thought to trigger an overproduction of melatonin for some people, creating a feeling of sluggishness and fatigue.

5. Infectious disease cycles

We know that winter is the cold and flu season, but why and how does this impact on our health holistically? The viruses that cause colds and flu thrive in colder temperatures due to slower decomposition, so they linger longer on exposed surfaces, increasing our chance of illness. It was originally thought that we catch more respiratory illnesses in winter because we are indoors together more often, making transmission more likely, but research has shown that cold temperatures themselves lower immunity in the nose and make us more vulnerable to catching viruses[9]. A drop in nasal tissue temperature of only 5°C reduced the immune response by nearly half. Cold temperatures lead to drier air, which can dehydrate nasal mucous membranes, interfering with the body's ability to defend itself from respiratory viruses.

Other than the low temperatures and damp associated with winter, lack of sunlight itself has a direct impact on our immune function. Research has shown that exposure to sunlight boosts our immunity by making immune cells move faster around the body, helping the body fight inflammation[10]. Without adequate access to daylight, this is another reason we are more susceptible to infectious diseases in winter and these conditions take a toll not just on our physical health but our mental health too. When the immune system detects the presence of an infection, it launches an inflammatory response that has an impact on the nervous system, leading to a range of outcomes dubbed as "sickness behaviour"[11], such as reduced movement and a desire to withdraw socially, both of which we know contribute to a depressed mood[12].

6. Increased appetite, decreased movement

Research has shown that there are seasonal influences evident in our diet and exercise patterns. We consume more calories in winter[13], our body weight peaks in winter[14] and our physical activity is at its lowest in winter[15]. Calorie intake and the tendency to move less, leading to greater weight gain in winter, may be a biological drive to bulk up in order to withstand the "food scarcity" historically experienced in winter. This could also explain why most developed societies show an increase in cardiac mortalities during the colder months. There are several mechanisms at play here. Cold temperatures have an impact on appetite, affecting how much we want to eat, what we want to eat and our feelings of fullness. Research shows we not only feel hungrier in colder temperatures, but we also crave energy-dense foods and feel less satisfied by our food[16].

7. Winter posture

We know the cold is aversive, making exercise feel less appealing, but less commonly appreciated is the effect that lower temperatures have on our muscular tension, posture and breathing, and the impact this then has on our psyche. What posture do you adopt when you go out into the winter gloom? We've all seen the ways the body protects itself against the cold – from wrapping arms around itself to conserve heat and a rounded spine to a downcast line of sight and often a clenching in the chest, shoulders, jaw and brow. Research has shown that the way we hold our bodies not only has a powerful impact on our state of mind and energy levels[17], but also plays a part in how we recover from a bad mood[18].

Specifically, studies have found that a tall, upright spine, open-hearted chest and a relaxed swinging action of the arms gives us access to a feeling of positivity, optimism and zest[19]. Conversely, the posture we adopt when we brace ourselves against the cold lowers energy levels, mood and makes it easier to recall negative memories[20]. It's also hard to breathe deeply in this body position and the mantra here is, *"When we breathe better, we feel better"*. You'll experience this for yourself in Step 4, which focuses on comfort (see page 104).

8. Financial burdens

The simple fact is, winter is the most expensive season in terms of the basic cost of living; the colder weather and darker days mean higher energy bills due to the gas and electricity needed to light and heat our homes and workplaces. We use on average 36 per cent more electricity in winter[21], on heating, lighting, tumble drying and running dehumidifiers. It is expensive keeping everyone kitted out in winter layers, boots and outdoor equipment and paying memberships for indoor exercise facilities. Plus, if we eat more in winter, it stands to reason that our food bill is also higher. We can also spend a fortune on cold and flu medications. Fuel economy is poorer in cold temperatures, so it is more costly running cars in winter. This collective financial burden can significantly add to our stress levels, hampering an effervescent mood.

9. Altered lifestyle choices

In addition to changes in our eating and movement patterns, cold, wet and dark conditions have a significant impact on the amount of time we spend outdoors. Exposure to Nature has serious benefits for our health and well-being and the effects are well-documented for attention[22], memory[23] and mood[24]. In the absence of the energy and mood boost we normally receive from movement and time in Nature, we tend to turn to compensatory behaviours for a feel-good hit – sugar, caffeine, alcohol, drugs and screens. And all of these have their own energetic tax that diminishes the quality of our sleep, adding to financial strain and generally making tomorrow harder.

Why hibernation mode feels hard

Seasonal affective disorder aside, winter's impact can be far more subtle: an increased need for rest and the desire to cocoon in search of comfort and warmth. This is hibernation mode and it is a very natural response to the season, providing us with time and space to reflect, restore and sustain ourselves when it's tough out there. Winter encourages us to come back to a more compassionate, intentional pace, honouring our internal fluctuations.

We've observed all the environmental, mental and physiological reasons why life feels harder in winter, but it's also a function of the hibernation mode itself presenting a unique challenge in modern times. There are cultural threads to the difficulties that winter presents. If winter calls us to slow down and reflect, this is hard for genuine reasons.

We know nothing blooms all year, so why do we human beings expect to have the same energy and performance all year round? We are not immune to the signs and signals from our environment and our hunter-gatherer ancestors would have altered their daily rhythm in response to hours of daylight and access to warmth. With the advent of artificial light and central heating, 24/7 communication access, and with social media showing us all the fun other people are having, we often plough on without considering how seasonal variations impact our daily flow. We treat ourselves like machines with infinite capacity, relentlessly pushing on, denying our right to biorhythms, to downtime, to an "off" switch.

The financial climate can make it feel like we need to work harder and longer to prove our loyalty and demonstrate our worth. While we might fancy an earlier night, a longer lie in, an afternoon nap, we can't always act on these impulses – we have deadlines, bills to pay and kids to collect.

While it's a totally normal desire to retreat, the pace of modern life and our associations with rest and productivity have us soldiering on as if nothing is happening around us, cursing ourselves for not being more bright-eyed and bushy-tailed and damning the weather for not being more conducive to what we feel is required of us.

It's more than the conflation of doing and productivity with self-worth, it's the fact that we are often deeply resistant not only to rest, but stillness, quiet and being faced with ourselves. Winter might call to us to reflect and recalibrate, but we've become so accustomed to the busyness and noise that this slowing down can feel alien, the quiet can feel deafening and the awareness of our inner worlds can feel overwhelming. Some people would prefer the distraction provided by self-administered electric shocks than to be faced with the cacophony of their inner world[25].

It's no surprise we've become so intolerant of pauses – spend just a few minutes consuming the video content on social media and you'll soon notice all the natural gaps in speech are edited out. In this world that demands our attention, requiring pithy, right-to-the-point information, we are becoming less skilled at delaying gratification. We want the quick fix and we want it now. It can be hard to slow down. It can be hard to sleep and rest when it makes us feel guilty. It can be difficult to establish healthy habits when energy and mood is low. We can feel lonely and isolated in our social retreat. We need a self-care plan to help us carve this delicate balance in response to the unique demands of winter. We're going to build that plan together next.

We know that the winter gloom can have far-reaching implications for our thoughts, feelings and choices. Given these conditions, we need antidotes to help us harness what our minds and bodies are calling out for.

Meet the 7 Steps
of winter well-being

1: Harness Light & Colour

2: Make a Healthy Movement Habit

3: Embrace Nature

4: Savour Comforting Rituals

5: Develop a Compassionate Pace: Sleep and Rest

6: Make Meaningful Connections

7: Practise Reflection

Using these seven steps, the pages to come will help boost your well-being in winter. Think of this as the nourishment that you need in life to function well. It may have similar building blocks to what you need in other seasons, but we're going to be more nuanced and allow it to take a shape that honours our fluctuating needs, resources and energy levels in winter.

Over the coming chapters you will be introduced to how the seven steps can help you thrive in the colder months, each with tangible practices to maximize your joy from this season. While there is an intelligence to their ordering, the steps are not sequential or hierarchical in nature. You can start wherever you feel drawn, safe in the knowledge that every step is taking you in the direction of feeling good in winter. Select at will

from this sustaining pick and mix, knowing that different things will motivate different people and what resonates for you will change over time too, so there is plenty of choice. Every day, the action can be tailored to your preference and needs.

Focus on what speaks to you now, leave for another reading the options that don't call to you in this moment. You may feel entirely different the next time you dip into these pages. Each year, your winter may be unique, depending on the other variables unfolding in your life at the time. Feel how these seven steps help you identify the support you need, while respecting your capacity for action, and remember, it is ok for this to change over time.

REFLECTION TIME ON THE 7 STEPS

Looking at these seven steps, what is calling you now?

What do you need to feel alive and at peace?

Can you think of ways you can factor those needs into your daily life? Don't worry if you're not sure – the coming steps are full of practical tips and tools.

This is just an opportunity to reflect on what you know already works for you.

What feels available to you right now?

Can you think of logical places you can schedule these commitments or pursuits into your week?

Make an appointment with yourself for at least one of these things or, even better, go and do it now!

1.

Harness Light & Colour

Daylight is in short supply in winter and the natural palette is one of greys, whites and browns compared to the riot of colour in spring. This step explores how we can cultivate our internal sunshine, using light and colour in our lives

There are simple adjustments we can make to our homes and how we choose to dress, as well as meditative practices to uplift us regardless of the external variables.

How to maximize natural & artificial light

There are many simple ways we can harness the power of natural light in our home environment. You might like to start with maximizing the amount of light that enters your home by trimming back vegetation around your windows, keeping the window area clear of objects or furniture and cleaning the windowpanes themselves. During daylight hours, keep your blinds open and consider investing in tie-backs for your curtains to allow for maximal benefit. The curtain fabric you use also has an impact, with light-coloured curtains or blinds reflecting the light, as opposed to darker hues that may feel cosy, but can make your home feel darker because they absorb the light.

In addition to drawing light in, you can strategically place mirrors opposite windows where light naturally falls, amplifying it and making the space feel larger and airier. White or off-white paint for ceilings and woodwork also reflects sunlight, making spaces feel more open, and gloss paint can also act like a mirror. Art and interior accessories made of glass or brass have the same reflective qualities and even the foliage of some house plants can bounce light into the room.

Artificial light is essential in winter and a careful investment in a variety of lights, such as floor and table lamps, wall lights and pendant lights, in addition to overhead lighting will give you a layering of options, depending on the amount of natural light available and how you are using your space. Place lights where you need them the most – either to highlight art or aesthetic features of your home or in places where light is needed for reading, working or creative pursuits. The lampshade material can create different effects too – sheer fabrics will fill the room with more light or opt for opaques to produce more of a cosy glow.

The choice of light bulb can also add a seasonal twist on lighting your home interior. Select higher wattage for areas requiring more brightness and lower wattage in lamps to facilitate more of a winter ambience. There's variety too in the colour of the bulb, with warmer tones cultivating more of a cosy feel.

You can use light as decoration to lift your spirits. Fairy lights aren't just for Christmas! Drape them on top of high bookcases for a gentle luminance or pop them inside a large round vase to make them a feature. Candles provide a soothing light with the added potential benefit of a scent you love. There is lots of choice here – from tea lights to hurricane lamps and candlesticks – to bring a cocoon of light to any relaxing activity. Adorn your home with artwork or photography depicting natural light and choose images of light, such as a sunrise as your screen saver or phone wallpaper.

Light makes a huge difference to our mood and mental clarity. For a kinder start to the day than your mobile phone alarm, invest in a dawn-simulation light to gently wake you. Ideally, set up your work station near a window where you can enjoy natural light and gaze out for an energy boost. We know that winter is costly in terms of energy usage, so for rooms not in use, remember to turn lights off.

How to infuse your day with colour

Just as you can accent your home with strategically placed light, you can use a pop of colour in your decorating to make your environment feel more nourishing. From a bowl of winter flower bulbs to artwork, soft furnishings or even your favourite mug, choose the tones that lift your spirits and consider allowing some seasonal variation. Blues and green might feel cooling in the summer, but in winter, think of the colours you might be feeling deprived of – yellows, oranges, reds and pinks – for their warming properties.

Avoid anything that you find heavy or dull. You can wear colour you love to lift your mood, too. Identify a few pieces in your wardrobe that bring you joy or add a slick of colour that makes your heart sing on your lips, your fingertips, a scarf or bag.

Practices to harness light & colour

Here is some quick, accessible inspiration to draw more of that precious winter light and colour into your life.

Sun meditation

When the sun is making her glorious appearance, get more than just your dose of vitamin D, use it to fill your energy bank. Take a walk or sit on a bench and bask in her rays, getting to know first-hand the joy of "apricity", the warmth of the winter sun. If it resonates and it's safe to do so, close your eyes and imagine there is a cord directly from the sun, attached to the crown of your head. Feel the transfusion of light coming straight to you from her rays, filling you up. Repeat the mantra: *"I keep turning my face to the light. She will always find me"*.

Morning daylight walk

Take a 20-minute walk ideally in the morning for maximal benefit for circadian rhythm regulation. This will help you feel more alert during the day and drowsier when it is time to sleep at night. Avoid wearing sunglasses if you're heading out during the morning so the light can enter your eye, because the known effects of light on circadian rhythms are mediated by the retina[1].

Enjoy a colour meditation walk

Head out into any environment – urban or natural – and set the intention to notice different hues. Robins, kingfishers, brilliant red berries and moss that appears luminous in the sunlight are among my favourite finds. But don't limit yourself to nature: many a heart-warming moment has come from colourful dog coats. Seek out architecture, vibrant front doors, unique clothing designs, bright wellies and rosy cheeks.

Savour a sunrise or sunset

Sometimes you get the sun, the moon and the stars in the sky at the same time. Keep an eye on the weather forecast for clear conditions and seek out the beautiful light shows unique to this time of year.

A MEDITATION ON LIGHT FOR EVEN THE DARKEST OF DAYS

Find a comfortable seat and settle in, knowing that you can move at any time to maximize your peace. Ideally sit with your spine tall, shoulders and arms relaxed, eyes closed, your face soft and perhaps a gentle smile at the outer corners of your eyes and lips.

In this practice we are going to use a "mudra" – a hand gesture from the yoga tradition. Placing our hands in different positions can have an impact on how our breathing feels, cultivating different energetic effects.

Have a little experiment for yourself and just see what you notice. If you place your palms upwards, this tends to make the inhalation feel more spacious, bringing with it a feeling of lightness and energy.

Alternatively, if you place your palms downwards, this makes your exhalation feel more robust, helping you feel stable and grounded.

For this meditation, we are going to use the "heart mudra": curl the tip of your first finger to the base of your thumb, touch the tips of the second and third finger to the tip of the thumb and extend the little fingers.

With your hands held in this gesture, palms facing upwards, settle into your seat and breathe freely.

What you might notice is this position of the hands makes it easier to breathe into your chest – the perfect antidote to the huddled, teeth-chattering posture winter brings us into.

Feel how spacious the breath is around your heart centre – enjoy this sense of freedom and ease, focusing your mind on the expansion of the inhalation and the gentle, effortless retraction of the exhalation.

Stay with this part of the practice for a few minutes or longer if it feels good to you.

If it appeals to you, staying as you are, imagine a light source in your heart – as an Antipodean, I love the image of the sun rising over the ocean, or you could choose an imagined fire or candle flame.

Choose whatever resonates for you.

Imagine it burning brightly in your heart, generating warmth, light, hope and peace. Perhaps it glows stronger with every exhalation.

Allow your mind's eye to settle here, basking in the glow for a few minutes, or as long as you can spare.

You have connected with your inner light, remember it is always with you, even on the darkest of days.

REFLECTION TIME ON LIGHT & COLOUR

How might you bring more sunlight into your home?

Are there tweaks you can make to maximize your use of artificial light?

~

Identify some favourite garments that you can use to infuse your day with uplifting colour.

~

Consider how you could use colour in your home interior over winter to boost your mood. Which colours are calling to you and how can you weave them into your life?

~

If you like the idea of the daylight or colour walk, can you schedule these into your day so they can become a regular feature?

Can you use part of your commute for this purpose?

~

Which of the meditative practices on light speak to you?

Where and when might you practice them?

2.
Make a Healthy Movement Habit

If the mere mention of movement has you flipping straight to the next step, I encourage you to stick with me. It is with my psychologist's hat on that I recommend this step to you, not in my capacity of personal trainer or yoga teacher. In my experience of helping thousands of people cultivate a movement habit, this might be the most effective commitment you can make to yourself – not only for your body but, most importantly, for your mind. This step, while about the nuts and bolts of moving in winter, is all about your mood.

Notice from the outset that this step is about movement, rather than "sport" or "exercise". Cast aside the notion that it has to be difficult, high intensity or that you need to be "good at it" to gain any benefits. This is all about finding movement that feels good to you in the winter months. It's about ways of moving that help to create warmth and help you feel alive, finding options that honour low-energy days and developing sequences that counteract the posture we adopt to steel ourselves against the cold.

In this step you will find all the movement inspiration to keep you moving outdoors, indoors, with friends and on your own, with a special focus on practices that support expansion, releasing physical tension and facilitate the kind of posture that lifts our mood and energy levels. This is not about gaining a six-pack or keeping the scales happy – this is about feeling even-keeled, anchored in perspective and armed with access to an excellent sense of humour; just the skills we need to navigate winter.

Before I take you through my favourite movement practices, let's brainstorm together a few different ways you can move your body. Get out a piece of paper and jot down all the movement options that come to mind, especially the ones that have a seasonal twist. Remember, all movement counts – from going to the gym to walking, dancing, playing with your kids and even jobs around the house, like vacuum cleaning. Can you think of some forms of exercise that get you warm and your heart rate up? Think as broadly as possible.

Or think along the lines of how you can work the movement into your daily routine. Is it possible to do your commute by bike? Or to get off the bus a few stops earlier and incorporate a brisk walk to work into your morning?

Take a look at your list and make sure there are some low-energy options, such as stretching or gentle core exercises, so you have something to choose from regardless of how you are feeling on the day.

Looking at your list, highlight a few different forms of movement you find enjoyable. Map it out with categories such as: at home, indoors, outdoors, solo, with company, for high-energy days, for low-energy days. Next mark any seasonal pursuits to keep up your sleeve. Take your planning one step further – what do you need to do to make this kind of movement happen? Is there equipment or kit you need? Would you like to find a buddy to enjoy this type of exercise with? Do you need to research a gym or class that you can get to? Get organized and identify windows in your day when you can get out and move, or stay in and move in a way that feels do-able today.

Practical movement inspiration

If you're still not sure where to start, even if you have drawn a complete blank on movement that feels good to you, relax, don't worry, I have you covered right here. Let me take you through the five movement rituals that see me through winter. In addition to getting all my layers on for frosty walks and jogs in Nature's beauty, I roll out my yoga mat (or stay sat on the sofa) and use one of the following five sequences at home.

For higher energy days:
Standing yoga sequence to strengthen and energize, and to help you break free from the "winter slump".

Mountain Breaths

- To begin, place a small cushion or rolled towel between your thighs and stand upright with your arms down by your sides.

- Squeeze the prop between your thighs and feel how this helps you ignite your thigh muscles, the perfect antidote to sitting.

- As you breathe in, stretch your arms out wide, palms facing upwards and raise them up above your head until your palms touch.

- Look up to your hands and as you breathe out, bring your hands slowly down to your chest, looking forwards and imagining that you are drawing fresh energy and light to your heart centre.

- Repeat 10 times.

Mountain Side Bends

- Keep the towel in place and prepare for an invigorating side stretch.

- Standing tall, with your arms down by your sides, breathe in and raise both arms overhead – this time keep your gaze forwards.

- As you exhale, take your left hand down by your side and reach your right hand up and over to the left, making a banana shape with the right-hand side of your body.

- Breathe in and raise your left hand up and bring your palms to touch overhead with your spine centred. As you exhale next, take your right hand down by your side, reach your left hand up and over and stretch the left-hand side of your body.

- Repeat 5 times for each side. This one might not look like much, but feel how it connects you with your core muscles – the same muscles that help us stand firm in the face of life's challenges.

- Notice if you feel a little taller and more poised following this exercise.

Dynamic Lunges

- Dispense with the towel and now stand with your feet hip-width apart. Prepare to feel alive with this one.

- Take a large stride forwards with your right foot, as far as you can comfortably step.

- Begin with your arms down by your sides and both legs straight.

- As you breathe in, slowly raise your arms forwards and upwards as you deeply bend your right knee. This is inherently unstable, so don't worry if you wobble, this is all part of feeling lively and responsive. To keep you anchored, firmly press your left heel back and down. It won't touch the floor but this action will help you balance.

- As you breathe out, lower your arms and slowly straighten your right leg again.

- Repeat 10 lunges on this side before shaking out your legs and taking 10 with the left leg leading.

- This sequence can feel intense but it's a great way to stretch the front of your body and strengthen the back of your body.

Dynamic Squat with Lotus Hands

- Another leg strengthener, but this one also creates flexibility in the hips.

- Start with your feet one-and-a-half times shoulder-width apart and your toes angled out away from you.

- In this sequence we are combining a squatting movement with a Lotus hand gesture to open the wrists and forearms – a great tonic after time spent tapping away at a keyboard.

- As you exhale next, bend your knees and sink into the squatting position. As you inhale, slowly rise back up to straight legs. When we descend into the squat, we form the roots of the Lotus: back of the hands touching and fingertips attempting to touch down to the palms. When we rise from the squat, we create the petals of the Lotus: base of the wrists touching, thumb and little finger touching and fingers spread as wide as possible to broaden the bloom.

- For an extra challenge, try lifting your toes throughout this whole sequence, activating the muscles deep in your lower abdomen.

- Repeat 10 squats paired with the Lotus hands, which is a great distraction from how hard your legs are working.

- The Lotus gesture reminds us that we have to plumb the muddy depths in order to grow. Dig deep in winter and know that in time you will bloom again.

Fold & Twist

- Take your feet twice shoulder-width apart and line up the outer edges of your feet so they are parallel.

- Take a deep breath in and then, as you exhale, hinge forwards at your hips into the fold. Soften your knees as much as you need to allow yourself to place your hands on the floor. If this feels uncomfortable, either use a stack of books or set yourself up in front of the sofa and place your hands on the seat.

- On your next breath in, place your right palm flat on your sacrum (your lower back), stacking your right shoulder on top of your left. As you exhale, replace the right hand to its original position. Next, as you inhale, place your left palm flat on your sacrum, turning your chest to the left. Take your left hand back down as you breathe out.

- Repeat the twist 5 times to each side and, for an extra chest opener, rather than hand to sacrum, stretch your hand up to the ceiling. Be guided by your comfort here.

- After your twists, spend 5 smooth breaths hanging out in the fold, allowing your head to drop towards the floor. Come up and out of this pose by bringing your hands to your hips and easing back up slowly with your next inhalation.

- Complete this sequence by coming back to **Mountain Breaths**. Take 5 of these to centre the energy you've created in your heart.

For medium energy days:

Floor-based yoga sequence that's also great to use as a method of unwinding after some outdoor movement.

Cat & Dog Tail

- Roll out a yoga mat, or using a rug or carpet will suffice, then come down to the floor on your hands and knees.

- Place your hands on the floor, shoulder-width apart with your fingertips spread wide and bring your knees, hip-width apart, beneath your hips. Breathe in to "angry" Cat pose with the chin pressed down towards your chest, scooping your navel to your spine and pointing your tail-bone down towards the floor.

- Feel how this stretches your upper back and strengthens your core muscles.

- As you exhale, draw your shoulders away from your ears, look forwards and point your tailbone skywards, coming into "wagging" Dog Tail pose. Notice how this strengthens the muscles behind your shoulders and gives the front of your body a stretch.

- Take your time alternating between these two shapes, moving into Cat with the in breath and Dog Tail with the out breath, 10 times.

Kneeling Side Plank

- From all fours, step your right foot back behind you, tuck your right toes under and then ground the whole sole of your right foot, pressing firmly down on the outer edge of your right heel.

- With care, float your right hand to your right hip and, imagining a wall behind you, stack your right shoulder on top of your left. Welcome to side plank, a balance pose that by its nature is inherently wobbly.

- Sense of humour engaged, consider raising your right hand straight up to the ceiling. For the adventurous, try taking 5 arm circles forwards, like front crawl, and then 5 back, like backstroke. Enjoy the freedom this creates for the right-hand side of your body.

- Come back to all fours and repeat, taking your left foot back.

- Once complete, try a few more Cat and Dog Tails and see if you have greater mobility in your spine now – proof that your yoga has a tangible impact!

Thread the Needle

- From all fours, take your knees wider apart than your hips and bring your big toes to touch. Breathe in and raise your right arm skywards, looking up to your hand.

- As you exhale, "thread the needle" by taking your right arm, with palm facing upwards, beneath your left shoulder and through, sliding it along the floor.

- Breathe in and unravel, taking your right hand skywards, then, looking up, exhale and thread the needle, taking your right ear to floor. Take 10 repetitions on this side before repeating with the left arm moving.

- Return to Cat and Dog Tail once more and feel the ease this has created in your upper back. Notice how full the inhalation feels there now.

Walking Downward Dog

- From all fours, tuck your toes under and slowly raise your hips so you are an inverted "V" shape – the Downward Dog.

- Rather than holding this pose in stillness, we're going to "walk the dog", alternately bending the knees, raising one heel up as you press the other heel down. There's no need to work too hard here, just feel the release in your calves and hamstrings and the strength this is building in your arms, shoulders and upper back.

- If this is new to you, it might feel intense, so start with a few on each leg and build to 10 each side, and hold in stillness for 10 breaths if this appeals to you.

Wide Knee Child's pose

- Give your arms a delicious break, coming back to all fours, knees wide apart, big toes touching.

- Sink your bottom back towards your heels, press your forearms to the floor and rest your forehead on the back of your folded hands.

- Hang out here for 10 breaths, letting your inner thighs and lower back soften and release with every exhalation.

Pigeon

- Coming back to all fours, slide your right knee towards your right hand and take your right foot over towards your left hand as far as it's happy to go. Inch your left leg back behind you, carefully lower your chest towards the floor, folding your arms and resting your forehead on your hands or making a tower with two fists.

- Be here and breathe calmly for 10 breaths, consciously relaxing your right buttock, hip and thigh.

- Repeat on the left side and, if you fancy, come back to Walking Downward Dog to release your legs.

Side Lying Thigh Stretch

- Come back to all fours and lower your body to the floor.

- Roll onto your left-hand side, stacking your right shoulder on top of your left, and your right hip on top of your left. This is another balance pose so engage your curiosity.

- Use your left shoulder to support your head and stretch out your left arm long like an anchor, then bend your right knee and catch hold of your right ankle with your right hand. Feel the powerful stretch this creates for your right quadricep (front of thigh).

- Hover here for 10 breaths before rolling to the other side.

Lying Prone

- Complete your practice with a few minutes of lying on your tummy, hands folded, forehead to hands. If you prefer to rest with your head turned, make sure you spend an equal amount of time with your head turned in each direction.

- Bring your big toes towards each other and let your heels flop apart. Notice how pleasant it feels to ground the front of your body, feeling the breath irrigate the back of your body.

- If Prone Lying doesn't feel good to you for any reason, please feel free to lie on your back instead. This is all about comfort so settle in and let yourself flop and drop for a few minutes.

For low-energy days:
A chair-based sequence to lubricate the joints and release tension. This is also good during the work day or while watching TV, either sitting on a chair or on the floor.

Neck Releases

- Gently rotate your head right and left, saying a slow "no" 5 times each way.

- Slowly lift and lower your chin, saying a big "yes" 5 times.

- Drop your chin to your chest and loll your head over to your right shoulder, then like a ragdoll over to your left shoulder, 5 times each way.

- Finish with a "turtle neck", pressing your head forwards, and then gliding your chin back, like a turtle poking its head out and back into its shell, 5 times.

Flamenco Hands

- Like a flamenco dancer, circle your wrists, making the movement as big as possible, with a liveliness right to the fingertip.

- Do 5 in each direction.

Ankle Releases

- Rotate your ankles in big circles, 5 times each way.

- Point your toes away from you and draw your toes back towards you.

- Do 5 of each, pointing and flexing, seeing if you can get your toes involved.

Shoulder Release

- Breathe in and squeeze your shoulders up to your ears and with a sigh, let them drop away, taking with it anything you no longer need.

- Take 5 "shrug and sighs" and repeat as needed throughout your day.

For when you don't feel like moving much at all:
A lying-down sequence that is also relaxing to do prior to bedtime.

Pelvic Tilts

- Ease into movement with a few pelvic tilts. Lying down on carpet, a rug or your yoga mat, arms relaxed by your sides, bend your knees and bring your feet flat to the floor.

- Breathe in and point your tailbone up to the sky, feeling this engage the muscles deep within your lower abdomen. As you breathe out, point your tailbone down to the floor, igniting the muscles of your lower back.

- Do 5 of each, giving yourself time to get going.

Dynamic Bridge

- Place your arms down by your sides, palms grounded and make sure your feet are hip-width apart, placed beneath your knees.

- Breathe in and raise your arms up and overhead to the floor behind you. As you breathe out, lower your arms back down by your sides and simultaneously raise your hips skywards. Inhale to lower your hips to the floor and raise your arms overhead, then exhale your arms down and your hips up.

- Take 10 of these, feeling the power of your thighs and glutes, and the heat this exercise creates.

Greet Your Abs

- Lie on the floor, knees bent, feet flat on the floor, but this time bring your palms flat to your thighs. Breathe in and let your whole body relax. As you breathe out, press your feet firmly to the floor and your palms down into your thighs.

- With each exhalation and press, you will feel your tummy muscles leap into action – enjoy that sensation but don't try to "work your abs". Focus your attention on pressing through your hands and feet and letting your abdominals get involved of their own accord.

- Repeat 10 of these, connecting with your core strength and personal power.

- Once complete, rest your hands on your tummy and take 10 calm breaths, noticing how much easier it is to relax after a little gentle exertion – making this a perfect pre-bedtime ritual.

Hello, Hamstrings

- Locate a scarf or use a tea towel to assist you with this hamstring stretch.

- Lying on your back with your knees bent and feet grounded, bring your right knee into your chest and hook the scarf over the ball of your right foot, pressing the right heel skywards.

- Slide your hands up the scarf so that you can get a firm grip and then straighten your arms. See how straight you can work your right leg and, if it feels ok, there is the optional challenge of stretching your left leg out, along the floor, keeping the heel flexed.

- Take 10 smooth breaths here before greeting your left hamstring.

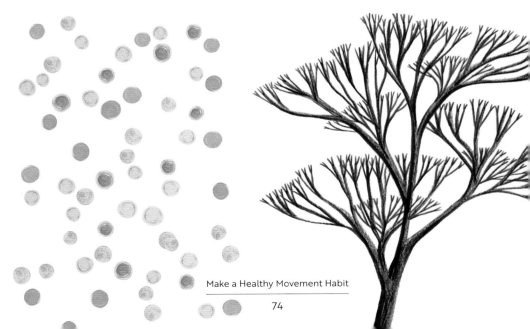

Make a Healthy Movement Habit

Lying Down Twist

- Let it all go with this restorative twist.

- Begin lying on your back with your knees drawn into your chest and your arms outstretched, level with your shoulders.

- Carefully lower your knees over to your right elbow, keeping your left shoulder firmly grounded. If it feels ok for your neck, turn your gaze towards your left hand or just look up to the ceiling.

- Stay here for 10 breaths, releasing the left-hand side of your chest and lower back, before coming back to centre and repeating to the left.

- Once both sides are complete, return to lying on your back, hands on your tummy and feel the energy and peace you have cultivated with this commitment to yourself.

- Give yourself a pat on the back for doing it even when you didn't feel like moving.

For no-energy days:

Welcome to your zero energy, zero motivation option – a restorative pose in stillness. Consider this permission to be human because we all have times like these.

Reclining Butterfly pose

- Think of this as your grown-up den-building practice and grab a selection of blankets, pillows and cushions in preparation for maximum comfort. If you have a bolster, this is ideal. If not, cushions will do.

- This is Reclining Butterfly pose, where we sit on the floor and place a bolster or series of cushions behind us to lie over and elevate your chest and head.

- Bend your knees with your feet together, let your knees drop out to the sides and bring the soles of your feet to touch, making the "butterfly". Place cushions beneath your knees for comfort and drape yourself in blankets.

- Snuggle in here and drop off, if you wish. You are getting a zero-effort release for your chest and hips, and the femoral artery is freed up to allow greater circulation to your legs.

- Nothing is required of you here, just let go and allow gravity to do the work for you. Stay as long as you wish.

Tips on how to make a healthy movement habit

Let's begin by acknowledging that our desire to move might be minimal and if our mood and energy levels are low, we need to be super gentle with ourselves when it comes to creating any new habit. Getting clear on your personal motivators can be a powerful place to start. What's in it for you? There are so many benefits to moving, but what speaks personally to you? Is it heart health, bone health, strong muscles, so your clothes fit you well, flexibility, for energy, to promote sleep, for an antidepressant effect, to reduce anxiety, to boost creativity and focus, to feel connected with other people, for longevity?

Don't just think of yourself in this moment, spare a thought for your Future Self too. We need to move now for our ability to balance and bounce back from slips and trips in years to come. We can protect our Future Self from the hazards of falls, which in later years can be genuinely life-altering. A powerful way to bring these benefits to light is to journal about how you feel before moving and then again after you've moved, plotting the changes you've observed. Check in with these entries to help encourage you to move when motivation is low – like a little love note to your Future Self, coaxing you into action.

When you're building a movement habit, it helps to have choice. Remember, you can always turn to the sequences in this step if other plans have fallen through. Brainstorm some primer statements so you always have a contingency plan articulated for you. Has bad weather scuppered your outdoor option? No problem, you have your home workout. Your friend cancelled on you? Easy, switch to your solo plan. No energy? Simple, use your restorative toolkit. No time? Relax, you have a few stretches up your sleeve.

Boost your accountability by signing up to a challenge, like Park Run, or download the free Strava app if you want to track your movement, connect with other people and cheer each other on. Find a buddy to work out with, a club you can attend, classes you can join and enjoy the social element. Fill in any gaps in your knowledge with expert help. Who can help you make movement a daily feature? Could it be a coach, personal trainer, yoga teacher or an exercise physiologist who plans a programme for you? Consider a physiotherapist or osteopath and make use of the plethora of online resources available to you too. Make sure you have what you need to be comfortable. The right kit for the weather conditions can make all the difference to how enjoyable outdoors movement is in winter.

Make sure you warm up for your body well before exercising. Simple joint mobilisations work well and the standing yoga sequence (see page 60) provides some good preparatory options. And my top tip for when the freezing cold makes your breath feel shallow while exercising outside – use the heart mudra to open the top lobes of your lungs (see page 50).

To maximize the mood-boosting properties of walking, swing your arms and lift your line of sight as much as possible. I know it can be treacherous and care needs to be taken in slippery conditions, but looking up will help you into a more expansive upright posture and increase your chances of seeing things that pique your curiosity. It's not just about movement – make sure you get adequate sleep, rest and recovery time too. Let there be a sigh of relief... more on that in the steps to come.

REFLECTION TIME ON A
HEALTHY MOVEMENT HABIT

You have your mind map of movements that appeal to you, you know the benefits and you've articulated what movement personally facilitates your life – now jot down one commitment to yourself around how you will use movement to help you thrive in winter.

If more come to mind, feel free to fire away, but keep it manageable and anchored in compassion.

3.
Embrace Nature

When I reflect on my childhood and how I spent my time, I remember lots of time playing outdoors, pottering in the garden, making mud pies, crafting perfume from leaves and petals, tending to my rabbits, exploring the local headland. Simple indoor fun involved board games, imaginative play with dolls and figures, chatting on the landline in the hall, endless hours of reading and watching cartoons in the morning that then paved the way for *Neighbours* and *Home and Away* in the afternoon as I grew older. Fast forward a few decades and the landscape of life for our children is vastly different. Granted, I don't think I'd be letting my kids ramble about clifftops, but it was a different time back then. Blackboards and books have been replaced by screens in the classroom. Modern life for many human beings, both young and old, has become so dominated by time on screens. We rely on them for work, study, connection, managing our lives and in our downtime, so much so that time spent in Nature is being squeezed out. When the elements feel hostile, and we feel that impulse to cocoon, we can become even more Nature-deprived. But it's so important that we make the commitment to getting outside. Our health and the health of our relationships depend on it. It takes diligence and planning, but it is so worth it. There is a glorious host of well-being benefits and life-giving skills developed by virtue of being in Nature.

The benefits of Nature on our well-being

Before we digest the research on the benefits of being in the great outdoors, I invite you to reflect on what Nature means to you and what you see as its personal impact on your well-being. What do you love about Nature? Where do you enjoy going and why? How do you feel when you've been outside? How do you feel when you haven't had a dose of Nature therapy for a bit? What are your favourite ways to imbibe the benefits of Nature in the winter months and have you been making space for this of late?

The health and well-being benefits of time spent in Nature, where we feel safe, are well documented. Let's take a look at the incredible rewards.

- We know that access to daylight regulates our circadian rhythms, helping us to feel more alert and productive during the day and sleep better at night. We also know that the vitamin D absorbed by the skin from sunlight is important for our bone health[1] and protection from developing cancers such as melanoma[2]. As we saw in Step 1 – Harnessing Light & Colour – there are mental health benefits from exposure to daylight too; when sunlight enters the eye, it affects parts of the retina that trigger the production of serotonin, improving our mood and helping us feel calm[3]. Our immune health[4] is boosted by sunlight too – activating immune cells by increasing their movement around the body.

- Fractal patterns, repeating patterns or patterns that occur on a progressively finer scale, are abundant in Nature – such as in snowflakes and coastlines. These help to bring the brain into a wakeful but relaxed state. Researchers have found that observing fractal patterns can reduce stress levels by 60 per cent[5].

- Exposure to the diversity of microbes in green space boosts our gut health[6]. Breathing in microbes found in soil, or absorption through the skin when digging with your hands in the soil, has been found to stimulate serotonin production[7], helping us feel relaxed and happier.

- Forest bathing has a number of health benefits. Breathing in scent from trees has therapeutic properties. When we breathe in phytoncides – the antimicrobial organic compounds emitted by trees – it gives a boost to our immune system[8]. We also get to breathe in lots of negative ions (negatively charged molecules) when we forest bathe. Negative ions have an anti-inflammatory property[9], reducing our oxidative stress that is linked with many chronic diseases, from allergies and asthma to cancer.

- Gazing at nature has been shown to potentially expedite physical healing and recovery from surgery[10].

- Trying to stick to healthy habits or resist temptation? Research has shown that time in Nature can even reduce cravings[11]. It can also boost our self-esteem[12] and confidence. Perhaps a dose of Nature might be the very ingredient you need in your goal pursuit.

- There are some seriously powerful stress-busting properties of time spent in Nature: it can reduce cortisol levels, lower your pulse rate, lower your blood pressure, increase your parasympathetic nerve activation (the "rest and digest" mode of nervous system activation) and reduce sympathetic nerve activation[13] (the stress response we all know as "fight or flight"). Other research has shown that a one-hour walk in Nature reduces activation of the amygdala (the brain's centre for processing emotions), showing that Nature is an effective means for restoring from stress. It also provides protection against future stress and a preventative measure against developing a mental health disorder[14]. Green space itself can provide a buffer against the negative health impact of stressful life events, promoting our ability to cope[15].

- Nature doesn't just provide us with a welcome break from screens, she actively refreshes our senses. When we engage "close-up" vision, like focusing on screens, our sympathetic nervous system is engaged. When we engage in panoramic vision, where we look out at the horizon or a broad vista, our gaze is dilated, allowing greater awareness of the periphery to the sides, below and above us, which is soothing for the nervous system[16]. If you can't see the horizon, look for any foliage because this also has a calming, restorative effect[17]. Even the presence of indoor plants in the workplace has been linked with greater productivity and employee satisfaction[18].

- Using nature as an anchor is a powerful way to hone our powers of observation and grow our mindfulness skills. Time in nature has been shown to enhance our cognitive performance, specifically improving our concentration[19], attention[20] and memory[21].

Embrace Nature

- Nature's positive impact on our emotional health is well-documented. It's a powerful antidote to anxiety: walking in Nature has been shown to dial down negative thinking[22] by reducing neural activity in the part of the brain responsible for anxious thoughts. It's also been shown to reduce hostility[23], sadness and anger[24] and be effective in alleviating feelings of loneliness[25]. It doesn't just help us manage the heavier emotions, it also promotes pleasurable feelings of happiness[26], joy[27] and awe[28] and can even help us feel more alive[29].

- Being in Nature not only physically helps us to relax, but it can also provide a wonderful distraction from a busy mind and our bulging "to do" list. Heading out into Nature has the potential to shift us out of doing more and into "being" mode, with plenty of natural phenomena to absorb our senses in a life-giving way. There's always something uplifting to attend to – be it sight, sound or scent. We harness this benefit when we use time outdoors as a means of enjoying an absence of striving and ambition, or a conscious break from problem-solving or decision-making.

- The healing power of Nature extends beyond the physical body and can also promote healing in our grief journey[30]. In addition to the soothing properties of being in Nature, many people report a sense of connection with loved ones through Nature – either returning to a place of significance, enjoying treasured past times or feeling a sense of continued relationship by observing Nature. The presence of white feathers or the appearance of robins are often interpreted as messages from lost loved ones, reminding us of their continued care and that the relationship goes on. I believe that my father visits me as a kingfisher, his first appearance on the day of his funeral, then after several months of no sightings, he bounded out on the common as a stoat, reminding me he can take any form. If this concept doesn't resonate, skip straight on by, but for many grieving people this can bring deep comfort and solace.

- Nature also feeds our relationships, improving our communication and deepening our bonds[31]. Research has shown that the parent-child communication was more responsive in a natural setting than indoors. This is something you've likely encountered yourself. It is easier to have open and honest conversations or broach challenging topics when you are out together in Nature. The simple act of walking side by side can make conversations feel less confrontational and the soothing benefits of the natural environment dial down the stress response, helping us connect, empathize and problem-solve together. Other studies have shown that exposure to Nature can make us more caring and generous[32].

Which of these benefits of Nature speak to you?

There are so many advantages of spending time in Nature, but what speaks to you? What will motivate you, bearing in mind this may vary in different moments? This purpose will help you don your layers and get out in Nature, regardless of the conditions. Make a note of what feels galvanizing to you.

- Improved sleep.
- Increased energy.
- Enhanced sense of being alive.
- Feelings of happiness, hope and awe.
- Diminished aggression and anger.
- Reduced stress levels.
- Antidote to depression.
- Anxiety relief.
- Better immune health.
- Deeper bonds and more effective communication.
- Confidence boost.
- Improved cognitive performance – better focus, accuracy and memory.
- Support through loss and change.
- Tonic for loneliness.
- Expedited healing.

Rituals to connect with Nature outdoors

Here are a few ideas for how to get out of doors and keep yourself motivated to get the most from Nature at this time of year.

Mindfulness walk

Head outside and leave your "to do" list behind. Focus on what you can see, with the option of taking photos to remember or to share your joy later. Seek out colours, shapes, textures, reflections in puddles, sunlight bouncing off wet roads or silhouettes of naked branches. Embark on a plant hunt, counting the different varieties you can see. There are wintry blooms to enjoy too – snowdrops always bring cheer, their sweet little heads nodding in agreement. Hunt for moss, lichen and mushrooms. What wildlife can you spot?

Sound meditation

What can you hear? If it's snowy, you're in for a treat. That crunch of untouched snow underfoot is so satisfying. If you have the chance to explore a frozen lake or canal, you might be surprised at the sounds available to you; the other-worldly ping when you toss chunks of ice onto the frozen surface, or the creaking it makes as the ice sheet melts. If not, the birds will keep you nourished. They can give you an incredible surround-sound experience. Running water is another soothing anchor and just the sound of the wind moving through the trees can be mesmerizing.

Awe walks

This is like a mindfulness walk but taking it to the next level. You are not only deeply immersed in the present moment and focused on your surroundings, you are paying close attention to things you may not have noticed before – large or minute. Be specifically on the lookout for things that cultivate a sense of curiosity or wonder, then immerse yourself in the experience of the joyful feelings that come in response to connecting with Nature. I love seeking out dew drops, looking for light and searching for wintry fractal patterns like spiderwebs, pine cones, snowflakes, frost, ice, leafless branches, seed heads, waterways or clouds. Keep a special eye and ear out for natural phenomena unique to winter! While many of us are not in the position to see the northern or southern lights, we could be lucky enough to experience "thunder snow" (just what it says on the tin – lightning and thunder during a snowstorm), or maybe you'll spot a nacreous, also known as "mother-of-pearl", cloud. This is more than just noticing Nature's beauty: this is basking in the glow of awe she brings – feeling the energy, inspiration, appreciation, perspective and hope. Take a friend to amplify the experience!

Savour the winter wonderland

Use the onset of winter to plan a visit somewhere you can enjoy these seasonal delights: skiing, snowboarding, snowshoeing, sledging, ice skating, building a snowman, constructing a snow shelter, snowball fights, snow-angel making, icicle hunting. Be a sleuth with snow tracking – look closely at prints and wonder what or who could have made them? Can you catch a snowflake on your tongue? Enjoy the sounds unique to this too – like creaking ice or the sound that snow makes as it melts from the treetops.

Sunrise or sunset meditation

Whenever you see the sun, appreciate the feeling of it on your body and drink it in.

Bird watching

Which birds are still around in the cold? I love the red kites wheeling overhead in the winter months. Robins often say hello and you can't beat the bolt of blue from the kingfisher, while goldfinches are a treasured spot. Back home in Sydney, I'd count upwards of 40 different types of birds on walks in my local area, but it's easier to spot and tell the difference between Antipodean birds like cockatoos and kookaburras. The birds in my new neighbourhood are titchy little things and they zip about so fast that I can't identify them, but I have fun trying – and you don't have to be able to name them to gain deep joy in seeing and hearing them. (Hats off to anyone who can tell the difference between a dunnock and a sparrow, which is on my bucket list of skills to master!)

Cloud gazing

What types of clouds can you identify? Or, if you prefer, free your imagination and spot freeform shapes with a companion. Have fun with your own weather predictions.

Nocturnal sensing

Take a night-time walk and engage your senses. Can you hear an owl? Are the foxes out? Enjoy how this fine-tunes your hearing, night vision and proprioception. Being in the darkness also stimulates the production of melatonin[33] – the sleep hormone – helping you wind down and feel prepared for sleep.

Star gazing

One of the benefits of fewer daylight hours is the increased opportunity to take in the starscape. Enjoy getting to know the night sky, watching planes and identifying constellations.

Moon gazing

When sunlight is in short supply, seek your sustenance from the moon. Keeping a moon diary can be an enjoyable way to get to know the lunar phases and plot any patterns in how you think and feel and the quality of your sleep. For thousands of years, various cultures and civilizations the world over have used the moon as a calendar and planned their activities accordingly. Jot down what you observe and see if any patterns emerge.

Forest bathing

Take a woodland wander. This is not about getting the heart rate going with exercise, this is about slowing down and connecting with Nature. Look up close at the trees, observe the light through the branches, the texture of the bark and breathe in the scents emitted by them. Enjoy taking it all in with nothing to strive for and nowhere else to be.

And now for a quick-fire round:

- Climb a tree or give one a hug.
- Take a bike ride.
- Garden – there's always something to do. Try planting bulbs for spring or deadheading the winter bedding.
- Backyard bug hunt.
- Feed the ducks.
- Visit a botanical garden.
- Try a cold-water plunge or some cold-water swimming.
- Fly a kite.
- Experiment with paper aeroplanes.
- Play an outdoor game, such as giant Jenga or Kubb.
- Gather around a bonfire and tell stories or roast marshmallows.
- Be a good citizen and beautify your neighbourhood with some litter-picking.
- Go for a drive and enjoy Nature from the warmth of your car.
- Savour a hot drink anywhere with a view.

WHAT TO WEAR TO ENJOY
NATURE IN WINTER

"There's no such thing as bad weather,
only unsuitable clothing."[34] *Alfred Wainwright*

It's not just about keeping warm,
it's about keeping dry, too.

Wear layers that you can adjust for comfort,
opting for waterproof fabrics for outer layers,
and wool rather than cotton for socks.

Invest in shoes or boots that keep your feet warm
and dry and provide good grip in slippery conditions.

Select bright colours or reflective gear for safety.

Protect your extremities, specifically your ears, nose,
fingers and toes, investing in thick socks, hat, headband
or earmuffs, gloves and scarf.

Safeguard exposed skin with a barrier of good
moisturizer and lip balm.

Pop some tasty treats in your pocket for sustenance
on the go and plan a warming reward on your return
– the anticipation of which will see you through.

20 ways to connect with Nature while *indoors*

Of course, even with the best of intentions and the most practical clothing, sometimes we still can't face leaving our warm bolthole to venture out into a grey fog, or a hailing downpour. Have no fear, here are some more ideas to get a Nature hit from the comfort of your cosy nook or nest.

1
Entice the natural world closer – perch at your window and see who comes by. Leave out seeds and insects for the birds, or nuts for other visitors. Look out your window as a circuit breaker when focus fades.

2
Bring the scent of Nature inside with candles or room sprays featuring your favourite aromas: pine for a wintry feel, or citrus or rose for something lighter.

3
Make some new floral arrangements.

4
Invest in house plants or grow an indoor herb garden.

5
Make a wreath, there are some great tutorials online.

6
Decorate a tree indoors.

7

Place talismans on the mantelpiece,
like pine cones and bare branches.

8

Create a photo album to savour wintry moments.

9

Make art with leaves, such as rubbings,
prints or collages.

10

Hang Nature-inspired art in your home.

11

Use Nature motifs in your wallpaper, curtains or linen.

12

Wear Nature-inspired prints or patterns in your clothes or PJs.

13

Choose natural scenes as your screen saver.

14

Read about Nature.

15

Listen to nature sounds inside – recordings abound, from birds
to water to rainforests, there is something for everyone.

16
Listen to others talking about it,
seek out a good environment-loving podcast.

17
Find a documentary that piques your curiosity.

18
Play games using Mother Earth as a theme – such as memory
pairs or jigsaws with an image of natural beauty.

19
Connect with Nature by enjoying seasonal cooking.

20
Visualize precious places – why not take a walk in a
sunny clime in your mind's eye? You are only limited
by the power of your imagination.

Embrace Nature

REFLECTION TIME ON NATURE

What are the benefits of Nature that speak to you? Make a mind map of these and use it as motivation when inclination is low.

෴

What are the barriers and how can you overcome them?

෴

Make a list of the ways you personally like to connect with Nature in winter. Use it as a well-being check list through the season.

෴

Reach out to a friend who may enjoy these pursuits with you.

෴

Are there new places you'd like to explore, different routes in your local area you could take or new outdoor activities you'd like to try?

෴

Keep a journal about these activities. Write about them using all of your senses: how you felt before you went out, during the experience and afterwards. Read these entries back to give you the motivation to go out again. Celebrate this beautiful commitment you are making to yourself and recognize the fruits of your labour.

4:
Savour Comforting Rituals

If you tune inwards at any time during winter, I am sure you will notice a desire for comfort. It is totally normal to want to snuggle in, seek warmth and protection from the elements. Let's not fight it! Let's work with it. The key here is to seek comfort in life-giving ways – ways that make tomorrow easier. This step is full to the brim with nourishing rituals, covering nutrition, ration and practices using touch, scent and breathing. It includes joyful ways to occupy your time, the nuts and bolts of creating a cosy nest in which to winter and how to alleviate common winter ailments.

Winter nutrition

We know that cold temperatures have an impact on our appetite, making us feel hungrier, less satisfied by what we eat and increasing our cravings for energy-dense food. It is totally natural to want to maximize receiving warmth and comfort from our food, but let's make sure that we have access to meals packed with nutrients to boost our immune health and mood. How can you allow there to be a seasonal twist to your nutrition, accommodating these natural shifts in hunger and what you fancy? What does healthy eating look like for you this winter, bearing in mind the other demands and challenges you're facing in your life? Are there some meals you could batch cook and freeze to make life easier? Check out the simple swaps you can make to meet both your desires and your nutritional needs.

If cravings are an issue, make sure you eat regularly – feeling "hangry" is the enemy of healthy choices and, remember, a dose of Nature therapy can help you keep cravings at bay too. Make sure you're getting plenty of lean protein that can keep you feeling fuller for longer[1]. Try these nutrient-rich foods to keep you feeling satisfied: wholegrains, Greek yogurt, avocado, nuts, seeds, eggs, beans, pulses, fish, fruit and vegetables. Plus, a sprinkle of red chilli pepper in your dishes can increase the sensation of fullness[2].

To optimize the nutrients available from our food, try to eat with the seasons. Seasonal food tends to be grown locally, potentially landing fresher on your plate. Food that's been grown in far-flung regions has had to travel significant distances and ingredients can lose nutrients while in transit and storage. Take a look at the country of origin of produce you find in your supermarket; for your best bet on freshness, seek out your local farmers' market.

Check out what's seasonal in your area, but here's a guide to some fruit commonly grown in winter: pears, apples, clementines, cranberries, passion fruit, satsumas, pomegranates, guava, grapefruit, cherries, kiwi, figs, lemon, oranges, apricots, plums, avocado. Vegetables include: cabbage, runner beans, spinach, swede, broccoli, turnips, artichoke, beetroot, carrots, butternut squash, celeriac, chard, celery, kale, leeks, parsnips, potatoes, pumpkin, mushrooms, brussels sprouts, onions, asparagus, peas and cauliflower.

Given that winter is cold and flu season, we want to improve our protection by eating foods that support our immune system and we need all the mood-boosting foods, too. Eating as much variety as you can of colourful fruit and vegetables will give you a good intake of antioxidants that help to protect against infections caused by bacteria and viruses. Foods rich in antioxidants include kale and green tea. Pumpkin and cranberries are a great source of vitamin C. Sprinkle some wheatgerm on your cereal for a dose of vitamin E and zinc. Onions and garlic help the immune system fight off cold and flu viruses, while oily fish, with its omega-3 fatty acids, is great for dealing with a number of winter ailments including dry skin, achy joints and the winter blues. Probiotics have also been shown to alleviate depression[3].

Ideally, we aim to get all of our nutrients from our diet, but there is evidence to support the effectiveness of these supplements in the treatment of depression: amino acids and their supplements – acetyl-L-carnitine, alpha-lipoic acid, N-acetylcysteine and L-tryptophan – have been shown to have antidepressant effects. Other agents with evidence for improving depressive symptoms include zinc, magnesium, omega-3 fatty acids and coenzyme Q10[4]. Evidence has also been found for vitamin D, methylfolate (folic acid supplement) and SAMe (s-adenosyl methionine) as being effective in the treatment of depression[5]. Always check with your doctor or pharmacist before taking new supplements.

Winter hydration

Don't be fooled into thinking that you don't need to drink as much water in winter compared to the humid summer months. Indoor heating can be a sneaky source of dehydration and we don't notice how much we perspire in winter underneath all our various layers. There can be increased respiratory loss of fluid in cold temperatures too when you lose water vapour through your breath. This is when you see a mist with your exhalation – that's fluid leaving your body.

Don't rely on your thirst – in cold weather, the body's thirst response can be diminished. When it's hot outside, we are much more likely to remember to take a bottle of water with us; we have to prime ourselves to keep up our water intake in winter. The preference for hot drinks might also mean that we are taking in less fluid over the course of the day compared to the water we happily gulp down in warmer months. Be mindful too that many of the warming drink options have caffeine and the rule of thumb here is one caffeine hit savoured daily, before midday, if we want to sleep soundly. While alcohol may feel like a warming option, it's also dehydrating and it's worth noting the impact that alcohol consumption has on your mood and the quality of your sleep, especially over the winter months.

The best source of hydration all year round is water, but it's appealing to have some seasonal variations – perhaps hot water with lemon might feel more invigorating, or add fresh mint, basil, ginger or rosemary to cold water. Remember, your fluid intake is not just what you drink, it's also in what you eat – another reason to make sure you're getting a gloriously colourful array of fresh fruit and vegetables.

Healthy comfort food swaps

Stews and casseroles instead of pies.

Protein balls instead of biscuits.

Broths instead of creamy soups.

Seasonal roast vegetables instead of fries.

Sweet potato mash, or add some carrot and cauliflower to the mash, instead of regular mashed potato.

Cakes and biscuits with spice instead of plain ones. A single gingerbread biscuit might be enough to satisfy that desire for something sweet.

Matcha, rooibos and chai tea, or golden milk (milk with turmeric, ginger, cinnamon and honey) instead of coffee and hot chocolate.

Comforting rituals using touch

When we receive caring touch, whether given to us by others or touch we extend to ourselves, it triggers the release of oxytocin, a hormone that is known to help us feel safe and calm[6]. Positive touch can reduce our blood pressure and lower our heart rate, and by reducing the release of cortisol it can support our immune response.

Touch can also be a powerful way to alleviate a sense of loneliness[7]. In addition to reducing stress, massage has the added benefits of increasing blood and lymph circulation, relaxing muscle tissue, reducing muscle stiffness and soreness, decreasing joint inflammation, improving flexibility and promoting sleep.

How can we harness the comforting powers of touch? Other than booking in to see your massage therapist, we can weave nurturing rituals of touch into our day via gestures, self-massage and snuggling with cosy textured props. The following pages feature a range of comforting touch rituals – try out a few and pick your favourites to come back to time and again.

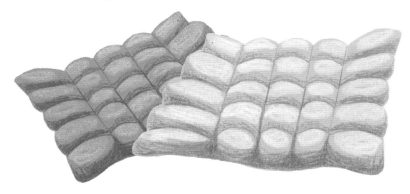

Savour Comforting Rituals

For when you're in need of comforting touch:
Seven tender gestures to experiment with

Hands on heart

- Place your hands on your heart, close your eyes and enjoy feeling the warmth of your hands on your heart centre. If it feels good to you, notice the beating of your heart and the sensation of your breath moving through your body.

- Repeat the mantra: *"Nothing fancy required. I give myself grace"*.

Cup your face

- Gently bring your palms to your chin and curl your fingertips round to meet your temples. Notice how nice it feels to be held: you *are* deserving of kindness and you *can* extend tenderness towards yourself.

- A beautiful antidote to negative self-talk, you might find that this gesture helps you cultivate more coaxing and encouraging words. If this is difficult, try using a pet name, like "honey", "sweetheart" or something given to you by someone you love.

- Repeat the mantra: *"I soften into this moment"*.

- Stay as long as you are able.

Cradle your eyes

- If you wear glasses, remove them.

- Rub your hands together to create heat, then place your palms over the whole eye socket, fingertips resting on your head. Allow your hands to completely block light from entering your eyes for a sensory rest.

- Feel the heat of the hands penetrate the eye area, soothing and restoring them.

- Relish that for the next 60 seconds – there is nothing else to be done.

One hand heart, one hand tummy

- Place one hand on your heart and one hand on your abdomen, it doesn't matter which, just whatever feels most comfortable for you. This gesture might help you feel more connected with both your heart and your gut instinct. You might also become aware of the sensation of your breath moving through your chest and your belly.

- See if you can allow the breath to move into both areas of your body.

One hand head, one hand heart

- Place one hand on your forehead and your other hand on your heart – as before, just as it feels natural for you.

- Feel how this calms a busy mind and perhaps facilitates a stronger connection between heart and mind. You are connected with what matters to you as a human being.

Hands on ears

- Place your hands gently over your ears, close your eyes and allow the outer world to drop away for a time.

- Enjoy the silence, the absence of stimulation, the sound of your breath and the feeling of containment.

- Repeat the mantra: *"I can be my own safe place"*.

One hand front of head, One hand back of head

- However it feels good to you, place on hand on the front of your head and the other hand across the back of your head.

- Feel the support this brings and how it quietens mental chatter.

- With this gesture, remind yourself that you are capable and you can be here for yourself.

For when you're in need of a comforting release:
Nine massages & releases using movement

Ears
Yes, even our ears carry tension!

- Holding onto the fleshy part of your ear lobe, gently tug out and down, repeat a few times, starting again as your fingers slide free.

- Mobilize the whole ear itself: with one hand, hold the top of the ear, with the other, hold the fleshy lobe, circle your ear 5 times one way, 5 times the other way, before repeating with your other ear.

- Starting at the top of your ears, with your thumbs and first fingers, imagine you are trying to unroll the cartilage, working your way through the whole outer edge down to the lobes.

Jaw
Sometimes a little bit of gentle exertion is the key to relaxation – far easier than trying to let go in stillness

- Try these 3 circling actions: circle your bottom row of teeth like you are making an "O" shape, 10 times one way and 10 times the other.

- Circle your bottom row of teeth around your top row of teeth, 10 times each way.

- Lastly, slide your bottom row of teeth forwards, slide it down, opening your mouth, then take it back behind your top row of teeth and repeat this elliptical action 10 times one way and then reverse it for 10.

- Feel this release tension in your face, mouth and jaw.

Eyes
Try this practice to refresh and lubricate your eyes (they tend to get dry from screen time, indoor heating and dehumidifiers)

- Imagine there is a clock face in front of you: squeeze your eyes shut and open them at one o'clock, squeeze them shut again and open at random at another time on the clock face. Make sure you visit each hour.

- If it feels good to squeeze them tightly shut, go for it, but just be guided by your comfort.

Neck
Ideally, this massage will involve you placing your fingertips directly on the skin of your collar bones, beneath or on top of your clothes

- Start by stretching your left arm out by your side, palm facing forwards and place your right hand at the centre of your collar bones.

- Firmly slide your right fingertips across your collar bone towards your left shoulder and turn your head to look right simultaneously, feeling this release your chest, neck and shoulders.

- Do this 3 times before repeating on the other side.

Throat
This one is called the "collar bone hang" and it needs contact between the fingers and skin over the collar bones for traction

- Begin with the chin down and nestle your fingertips into the inner edge of the collar bone at the centre of the chest. Secure the skin with your fingertips (as if you're a rock climber hanging on for dear life) and lift your chin slowly skywards, jutting your lower teeth forwards to get maximum stretch.

- Repeat a few times with the hands placed at the centre before moving your hands further apart towards the middle of the collar bones – repeat 3 times with this placement.

- Finish with opening and closing the mouth a few times and feeling the freedom you've created.

Savour Comforting Rituals

Hands
This one is called the "alternating hand clasp and squeeze" and it will warm your hands, aid circulation and build grip strength

- Place one hand on top of the other as if you are clapping and wrap your fingertips around your hands, squeezing them, then place your other hand on top and squeeze.

- Repeat this alternating clasp and squeeze as quickly as you can, 10 times each way and feel the warmth it creates. Notice how easy it is to relax your arms after this exercise.

Hands & mind
This second hands sequence is slightly more involved than the one above, to benefit your mind as well as your body

- Interlace your fingertips and squeeze your hands together.

- Change the interlace so the other thumb is in front and squeeze. Repeat the alternating interlace and squeeze, noticing how hard it is to think about anything else at the same time – the perfect antidote to sticky, unhelpful thoughts.

- Try this 10 times each way or more if it's really useful.

Wrist & arm release
Your hands are so often busy, let go of the tension this creates with this stretchy movement sequence.

- Start with your arms straight out in front of you, palms facing each other.

- Take one arm on top so your forearms are crossed, turn your thumbs to point down, then catch hold of your hands by interlacing the fingertips.

- Keeping your hands joined, draw them in and towards you and back out again, feeling the stretching sensation for your wrists and arms.

- Repeat 10 times, then begin again taking the other hand on top. Finish by giving your hands a little shake to release them, consciously flicking off anything you no longer need. Let it leave the building.

Foot release
Great for achy, cold or tired feet

- Get comfortable in a position where you can reach your feet, whether that's sitting on the floor or in a chair, and take off your socks.

- For one minute, with both hands, squeeze firmly your foot, moving across the whole surface area – the toes, the arch, the heel, top and bottom.

- Once complete, compare the difference in colour and temperature between your feet and then balance things out by attending to the other foot.

- Next, mobilize your toes. Starting with the right foot, hold onto the big toe with your left hand and the second toe with your right hand and move the toes up and down, making the movement as big as you can – 5 times or so will do. Then hold onto your second toe with your left hand and your third toe with your right hand and repeat. Continue so all the toes get a turn and repeat on the other foot.

- Lastly, wake up your feet with this squeeze. Interlace the fingers of your left hand with the toes of your right foot. This will be tricky to do! As much as possible, get the fingers as low down between the toes.

- Now squeeze your toes using your fingers for 5 seconds and then squeeze your fingers using your toes for 5 seconds. Repeat 3 times before freeing the foot and changing sides. Notice how much more dexterous your toes feel after this practice. Perhaps you might feel more grounded when you come to standing, too.

Whole body practices
Some simple ways to release your whole body

- Take a bath and add some magnesium bath flakes for their anti-inflammatory properties.

- Use an exfoliating product in the bath or shower to buff away dead skin cells and feel alive. Rub in body lotion or massage oil and, while you're at it, say some nice things to your body. Repeat the mantra: *"Thanks for carrying me today",* or *"I appreciate you".*

- Try brushing your body with a natural stiff-bristled brush before your bath or shower once or twice a week. This also has an exfoliating effect and stimulates the lymphatic system. Remember to brush upwards along your limbs and give your brush a good clean on a regular basis. Again, don't skimp on pleasure! Be guided by your comfort (this might not be one for sensitive skin).

- Get your hygge on and follow the Danes by adorning yourself in woolly socks, chunky knitwear, cosy blankets and comfy clothes.

- Invest in a weighted blanket, which research shows can be effective in reducing pain[8], anxiety[9] and insomnia[10]. Snuggle up on the sofa with it or, if it feels resonant, use it to anchor yourself in bed as you sleep.

- Confession: one of my great joys of winter is being able to leave the house without wearing a bra. Whatever form it takes, relish your comfort!

Rituals using scent

Think of all the delicious ways you can invite the joy of scent into your day. Seek out your favourite body lotion, hand cream, bath and shower oil, perfume, room spray, candles, lavender bags... Notice the aroma of your beverages and food and, when you're outside, draw in the crisp fresh air and the scent of nature with all its immune-health-supporting properties.

Nothing beats the scent that you personally find resonant, but perhaps you've noticed a seasonal aspect to fragrance you enjoy, too. Different scents have different qualities and you might like to explore ones that create a feeling of warmth and cosiness. Spicy fragrances such as cardamom, cinnamon, clove, star anise or nutmeg might resonate in winter, while woody scents like cedarwood, sandalwood, patchouli, vetiver, oakmoss, pine and musk evoke a sense of fireside memories.

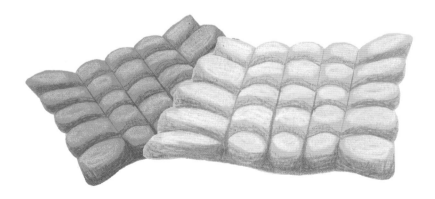

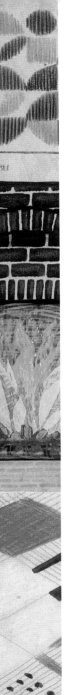

Breathe better to feel better

How we breathe has a profound effect on the state of our nervous system functioning. When our breath is calm and spacious, it is a cue to our nervous system that it is safe to relax. We can cultivate a feeling of peace, wherever we are, by smoothing out the breath. Even a single relaxed breath can be enough to shift us out of the stress response and back into "rest and digest" mode. Learning how to breathe well throughout your day not only helps you manage your stress levels, but it can also be the key to promoting better sleep at night. The inability to relax is one of the greatest barriers to sleep... so learn to breathe well and this will pay dividends around the clock.

Breathwork basics – what is good breathing?

Contrary to what you may have read about breathing, you don't have to employ fancy strategies to develop the ability to breathe well. What we are aiming for is a relaxed breath in, where there is a sense of expansion across your whole torso in all directions, and a gentle and effortless retraction back to your centre with the exhalation. The movement of the breath isn't just contained in the lungs – a natural inhalation will involve expansion in the chest, collar bones, side of the body, upper back, mid back, lower back and abdomen. Try the movement sequences in Step 2 (see pages 60–76) and feel how these stretches help free your breath into all areas of your body.

The more expansive and relaxed, the better. Notice the impact that the cold weather has on your breathing – it tends to make it short and shallow, our posture hunched making it hard to take a deep breath in at all. This shallow breathing can make us feel anxious and stressed so try the stretches in Step 2 to relax your shoulders, open your chest and explore the following breathing practices. Commit to practising the ones that feel good to you daily, some only take a few seconds!

For when you need to let go of winter tension:
Candle breath, the perfect winter breathing ritual

- Couple this with a cup of tea or as you sit down to a steaming hot meal.

- Breathe in through your nose, savouring the scent available to you and breathe out through pursed lips as if you are gently cooling your cuppa.

- Repeat just the once if that's enough to help you soften, or repeat as many times as you like to find your pocket of peace.

For when you want to feel centred:
Alternate nostril breathing, to balance the energizing and soothing effects

- This practice involves closing off one nostril and breathing in and out through the other nostril, before changing nostrils. For obvious reasons, this is one to practise when you are free of congestion, and it's good to blow your nose before starting! Research shows that breathing through the right nostril stimulates the sympathetic nervous system, which has an energizing, activating effect. Breathing through the left nostril, meanwhile, stimulates the parasympathetic nervous system, which has a soothing and calming effect[11]. By directing the breath evenly through both nostrils, this practice creates a balancing effect for the nervous system, helping you feel calm and alert[12].

- Find a comfortable seat where you can keep your spine elongated and shoulders relaxed.

- Begin by breathing in and out through both nostrils.

- Then, using the thumb or pinky finger of your dominant hand, close your right nostril. Allow the remaining fingers to lightly curl in towards the palm and let your other hand relax in your lap, palm facing upwards. Inhale through your left nostril.

- Remove your hand and repeat the gesture to close off the left nostril with your thumb or pinky finger. Exhale only through your right nostril.

- Keeping the left nostril closed, inhale through your right nostril.

- Close off your right nostril and exhale through your left nostril. This is one round.

- Aim for up to 5 minutes of this practice, always finishing by exhaling through the left nostril. Try to make the breath as even as possible through both sides, helping to create a relaxed focus.

For when you want to release physical and emotional tension:
Lion breath, to free up your face, jaw and throat

- This cathartic breathing practice helps to tackle emotional digestion, releasing resentment, frustration or anything that's hard to put into words.

- Breathe in through your nose and exhale through your mouth with the tongue extended as far out of your mouth as possible.

- Repeat 3 to 5 times, as needed, releasing anger and other irritations without doing harm.

For when you want to pitch up and feel poised:
Ujjayi breathing, to soothe and anchor

- This practice, also known as "victorious breath", has a gently heating effect and can feel empowering and galvanizing. The subtle sound and sensation provide an additional anchor for the mind, helping you to stay focused on the breath. It also helps to elongate the exhalation, which is soothing for the nervous system.

- Gently close off the back of your throat a little, as if you are saying the sound "ha".

- With your the back of your throat partially closed, and your mouth fully closed, breathe in and out of your nose, creating a soft "ha" sound like the ocean. Nothing forceful or loud is needed here, just a soft internal "ha" sound.

- Use this to accompany your chosen movements from Step 2 (see pages 60–76) or on its own while seated or standing still and gazing out of the window.

- A few minutes of this will help you feel relaxed and ready.

For when you'd rather move with the breath than sit in stillness:
Book openings, to focus on movement

- Sometimes working with the breath in stillness might feel uncomfortable, especially during times of worry or anxiety. If you've experienced this, you're not alone. The key here is to pair breathwork with movement. You are aiming to make the breath more spacious, but while focusing your mind on movement, rather than trying to deepen or change your breath in any way.

- Set yourself up on the floor, with a cushion or pillow to support your head. Lie on your right-hand side with your arms stretched out, level with your shoulders, and your knees bent, level with your hips.

- Breathe in through your nose and peel your left arm away, raising it up to the ceiling and back towards the floor behind you as far as it feels comfortable to go. Watch your left hand with your gaze, turning your head as your arm moves. As you exhale, slowly return your arm and head to their starting positions. Imagine that the inhalation and arm movement are like opening the pages of a book and the exhalation is like closing the pages.

- Do this 10 times on one side before rolling over to the other side and repeating it with the right arm moving.

- Once complete, lie on your back with your knees bent, your feet flat on the floor and your hands on your chest or abdomen, one on each, or out by your sides. Enjoy 10 breaths here in stillness, if it now feels good to you.

Life-giving ways to occupy our time

While squirreled away from the elements, we need some wintry mood-boosting activities to pass the time. Whenever a spare moment arises, loneliness looms or you need a feel-good hit, take a peek at the suggestions below and select your tonic.

Laughter

Create a resource identifying your favourite comedic inspiration and refer to it for quick direction to something uplifting. This could be a note on your phone or mapped out on a single page. Sometimes we need reminding of our favourite TV shows, films, books, podcasts, TED talks, apps, guided resources and YouTube channels. Ask your friends for theirs and share your gems with each other.

Play

Play is not just for kids! In winter, dig out your favourite jigsaws, playing cards, board games, inspirational decks of cards, sudoku or brain-teaser puzzle books and and keep them somewhere handy for a regular dose of light-hearted downtime.

Creativity

Winter provides us with a beautiful opportunity for creative expression. Try knitting, crocheting, sewing, scrapbooking or baking. If the inclination strikes, challenge yourself with developing a new skill, such as learning a new language or hobby, and feel how this prevents you from stagnating.

Music

When energy is low and you want to receive a mood boost, lie back and listen to your chosen playlists. Create different lists for different moods so you can simply press play. Bring out your instruments and get creating too. Singing counts and, just like movement, you don't have to be good at it to reap the benefits.

Making your cosy nest

Given all the time we spend indoors in winter, we need to make our nest as cosy and inviting as possible. This is not about Marie Kondo-ing our entire home: let's respect the energy levels and aim for a good declutter or simply make a cosy corner. There are two essential features to making our nest as conducive to our well-being as possible and these are warmth and dryness.

You may have experienced the daily battle with condensation on your bedroom windows and felt overwhelmed by the threat of damp and mould. This can feel like a time-consuming daily event and perhaps you're aware of the health risks posed too. It can make winter a stressful and depleting time, but there are some simple strategies that can make all the difference.

Condensation forms when warm air hits colder surfaces like windows and walls, and this warm air can come from cooking, bathing and showering, boiling the kettle, using the tumble dryer, drying wet clothes inside and breathing at night. Where condensation gathers, damp can develop and mould can grow. Neither make for a life-enhancing environment to winter in; damp and mould produce allergens, irritants, mould spores and other toxins that are harmful to our health. Even without the presence of visible mould, dampness on its own poses health risks.

Excessive moisture can promote the growth of mould and fungi, dust mites, bacteria and viruses. Prolonged exposure can be very harmful to health. Damp and mould are dangerous for anyone, but the risks are even greater to young children, older adults, people with existing health conditions, especially respiratory conditions, or those with weakened immune systems. Most people come into contact with the harmful substances produced by mould and damp by breathing them in, so the effects are primarily experienced in the airways and lungs. However, other health consequences can include eye irritation leading to conjunctivitis, eczema, fungal infections and poor mental health[13].

Simple ways to reduce moisture in the house:

- Turn the kettle off immediately after boiling so it doesn't continue to emit steam into the room.
- Use pan lids while cooking to trap steam.
- Use the extractor fan when cooking, even when boiling water on the stove.
- Keep the kitchen door closed while cooking to prevent moisture distribution.
- Install an extractor fan in the bathroom and keep the door closed while bathing and showering to trap moisture. Afterwards, open the window a crack to allow steam to escape.
- Squeegee the glass of shower walls to reduce moisture.
- Open trickle vents in doors and windows to allow better ventilation. I know this allows precious heat to escape, but we want to be heating a dry environment, not wet environments that are a breeding ground for mould and bacteria.
- Make sure you have good insulation in your walls and roof to keep heat in and allow for these means of ventilation.
- Keep furniture away from external walls to aid circulation and prevent pockets where mould and damp can develop.
- Use the tumble dryer rather than drying clothes on the radiators – although this obviously has cost and ecological implications, too.
- Invest in a dehumidifier and keep condensation at bay. These can be surprisingly energy efficient, with the added benefit of helping preserve heat.

Ways to conserve heat in your home:

- Keep your heating systems well serviced and maintained so they are maximally effective.
- Bleed radiators once a season to make sure they're energy efficient.
- Move furniture away from radiators to make sure heat is free to circulate.
- Insulate your water pipes to save energy and reduce heat loss.
- Draught-proof your windows and doors.
- Keep doors closed and focus heat in the rooms that are regularly used.
- Turn radiators down or don't heat rooms that are unused.
- Maximize heat captured from the sun by having window treatments wide open during daylight hours.
- Close the curtains when the sun has gone down.
- Opt for heavyweight curtains to keep cold out and reduce heat loss.
- Cosy up your home with rugs to insulate the floor and blankets on the sofa for additional warmth.
- Use extra heat sources in the rooms you need warmth in the most, without adding to the heat of the whole home.
- After cooking with the oven, leave the oven door open to use the heat generated to warm the house, keeping pets and children safe, of course.

REFLECTION TIME ON COMFORTING
NUTRITION & HYDRATION

*What does eating and drinking typically look like for you
at this time of year?*

∼

*Are there any tweaks you'd like to make to your nutrition
or hydration? Remember, if you'd like to create any change,
aim for small incremental adjustments.*

∼

*Address just one meal of the day at a time, snacks, or your
hydration. Integrate that habit before embarking on the
next wave of change.*

REFLECTION TIME ON
COMFORTING TOUCH & SCENT

*After experimenting with this smorgasbord
of comforting touch exerises, make a mind map
of the different parts of your body with accompanying
soothing practices.*

~

Add you own to the pick and mix provided in this book.

~

*Make a note of your favourite winter scents and
jot down how you might enjoy them.*

REFLECTION TIME ON BREATHING PRACTICES & MAKING A COSY HOME ENVIRONMENT

Pause and notice how the cold impacts on your ability to breathe and observe any patterns in how this affects your mood, energy and thinking.

～

Give breathing practices a try and jot down how you felt before and after them. Note which ones appeal to you, why they felt beneficial and write down when they would be useful.

～

In addition to drawing in light and using colour in your home to lift your mood, what tweaks can you make in terms of managing condensation and heat to maximize your comfort?

～

Which area of your home needs a declutter?

～

Where can you create a cosy nook for yourself to retreat in?

5:

Develop a Compassionate Pace: Sleep & Rest

While it might be nice to curl up like a brown bear and sleep for months until the sun is back in action, modern life simply doesn't allow us to check out – and even if we could, it wouldn't be healthy for us. This step is all about establishing a compassionate pace: how we can tweak our expectations of ourselves in winter and meet our increased need for rest and sleep. We'll look into how we can promote the quality of our sleep so we feel more refreshed, rituals to start the day with zest, different ways that we can rest during the day when we run out of steam and simple strategies to keep us alert when there isn't time for that desired nap.

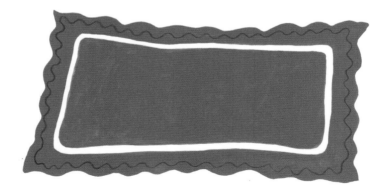

Winter calls to us to slow down, but as we've already observed, this is no mean feat when there is so much noise about productivity, stacks of stimulation, not to mention our bulging "to do" lists. There is a difference too between slowing down and grinding to a complete halt through burnout.

How can we gently alter our pace in this season? Take your pick from here:

- Slow, smooth exhalations.
- Repeat the mantra: *"I have all the time I need"*. Even if your mind argues with you, it's more relaxing to repeat something positive than statements of lack.
- Chew your food slowly and deliberately.
- Take small sips of your beverages and savour the sensation of swallowing.
- Take slow, steady steps, noticing how it feels to alter your pace.
- Slow down your speech.
- Turn up your listening skills.
- Solo task wherever possible. Relish the joy of doing just one thing at a time.
- Green-gaze out of the window.
- Watch the birds.
- Take in the cloudscape.
- Slow hugs.
- Screen breaks.
- Give caffeine, sugar and booze a wide berth.

Guidelines on being sedentary

Remember, this is about an altered pace over winter, honouring a lower mood and energy levels while still getting the movement that we need for our mental and physical health. It's not just that movement is good for us, the truth is that being sedentary for long periods of time has its own dangers. We want to strike a balance between time to flop and drop, and a commitment to moving our bodies.

- **Why do we need to get up and move?** Here's a reminder: movement aids our digestion, immune function, circulation of blood and lymph; we need it for the health of our muscles, joints and bones, for our mental health and for access to better sleep.
- **What are the risks of being sedentary for too long?** The effects of prolonged sitting on our health are so significant that it has been likened to the dangers of smoking. Research shows that sitting for too long is linked with obesity, heart disease, diabetes, Alzheimer's, anxiety and some cancers[1].
- **How often do we need to get up?** Ideally, we break up time spent sitting every 30 minutes. Nothing fancy is required – just get up, move about or have a stretch, then carry on.

If you need movement inspiration to break up sedentary periods, you will find it aplenty throughout this book (see pages 56–81). Take your pick!

Sleep, glorious sleep!

The question is, now that we know we need more sleep in winter[2], how can we meet that requirement? And how much sleep should you get as an individual? The guidelines on sleep are that healthy adults need a minimum of seven hours of sleep daily, though some people need up to nine hours of sleep[3], in particular young adults, anyone recovering from sleep debt and individuals with illnesses. Adults over the age of 65 may need up to only eight[4]. What's interesting is how your needs change with the seasons. It's normal to require less sleep in summer and more in winter, but how do you know if you're getting enough? The hallmark of good sleep is waking naturally (without an alarm) and feeling refreshed.

- **How many hours of sleep do you need to feel well-rested in winter?** Knowing we sleep in 90-minute cycles and have a greater chance of waking up feeling refreshed if we complete a sleep cycle, ideally we'd aim for five or six cycles, which is seven-and-a-half hours or nine hours.
- **What is your ideal bed time and rise time during winter?** Take into account the time it takes to fall asleep or get back to sleep as well as the number of sleep cycles. Where possible, consistency is best, Monday through to Sunday – but if you have a sleep deficit, catch up wherever you can.
- **Prioritize decent sleep.** It is the cornerstone of our well-being. When you feel well-rested, what does that give you access to, or what does it allow you to be? When you are sleep-deprived, what does it cost you?

Write down three reasons why it's not just ok, but it's necessary for you to allow yourself to meet your sleep needs.

Top tips to enhance the chance of good winter sleep

Before we begin, we need a caveat here. You can make all the supportive, healthy choices and still not achieve your desired amount of sleep. To dial down stress about wakefulness at night, let's shift the goal from hours of sleep to hours of rest. While we can't make ourselves sleep, we can cultivate the ability to rest – and rest is just as good.

Prepare your environment

Prime your mind and body for switching off by making your sleep environment a calming, relaxing sanctuary.

Create a cave-like retreat

A cave-like environment, think dark and cool, will be most conducive to sleep. Make the most of the lower temperatures and longer nights in winter and enjoy sliding into bed in a cool, dark room to get cosy. One of the mistakes we commonly make in winter is overheating our home at bedtime. To initiate sleep, our core body temperature needs to drop, so making the bedroom roasty-toasty interferes with our ability to fall asleep[5]. The ideal temperature for sleep is 16–18°C (60–65°F), so check your heating schedule and adjust accordingly.

Consider temperature changes

Both our body and ambient temperatures can fluctuate through the night so, rather than just one thick covering, having layers of bedding to adjust for comfort can be helpful. If you co-sleep, you could even consider having separate bed covers so you can better meet your individual preferences. This is particularly important if you're in the midst of perimenopause. Warming the feet can promote sleep by helping the core body temperature to drop[6], so wearing socks might be another option to maximize comfort and sleep.

Dimmable lights

We can prime ourselves for sleep by tailoring how we light our homes. It's not just the light emitted from screens that scuppers melatonin production, delaying feelings of drowsiness, the artificial light in our homes contributes too[7]. Darkness triggers the body to produce more melatonin, which signals to the body that it's time for sleep, whereas exposure to light reduces melatonin production, signalling to the body that it's time to be awake. Having dimmable lights allows us to tweak them according to our needs – brighter in the morning and during the workday, then dimmer in the hours before bed. Incorporating multiple light sources means we can layer our light, turning on cosy lamps in bedrooms and living spaces and leaving the more powerful ceiling lights off. Using plug-in hall lights during the night can help us avoid turning on bright bathroom lights, allowing us to stay sleepy.

Keep the air flowing

Air quality in the bedroom impacts on our sleep too. Research suggests that having a window open for air flow is important for good quality sleep and has the added benefit of boosting your cognitive function the next day[8]. Humidity in the bedroom is another factor, with more humid environments making it harder to sleep as well as adding to the risk of encouraging mould growth and dust mites. One of the great benefits of running an eco-friendly dehumidifier on night mode is that its white noise can be soporific. The ideal indoor humidity is between 30 and 50 per cent[9] – below this range can be problematic when you're fighting off a cough or cold because dry air can exacerbate the symptoms of both.

Clear the room

Keeping your bedroom free from dust, clutter and technology will create an environment perfect for sleep too. The clincher here is making it a space that feels calming, a place that you associate with relaxing and, ideally, a work-free place.

Prime yourself during the daytime

Other than environmental tweaks, lifestyle choices have a huge impact on sleep quality. If you want to promote the chance of good sleep, commit to daily exercise, get your 20-minute dose of natural light in the morning, be mindful of your caffeine intake (one caffeine dose prior to midday), avoid large stodgy or spicy dinners or eating late, abstain from alcohol and enjoy a pre-sleep routine free from screens before going to bed.

Pre-bedtime rituals to prepare your mind and body for sleep

Once you've prepared your space and body for a good night's sleep, take a bit of time to look at the hour or two immediately before your bedtime. One of the mistakes we commonly make is spending our whole day in "go, go, go" mode and then just expecting ourselves to be able to switch off when our head hits the pillow. Calming activities before bed, some of which take as little as five minutes to do, can provide the necessary segue to rest, paving the way for sleep to come.

A hot shower or bath

Unravel physical tension with a hot shower or bath, after which your body temperature drops, helping to initiate sleep. Time it 1–2 hours before bed for maximal benefit[10]. Even a 10–15 minute soak will promote sleep.

A gentle yoga routine

Release your mind and body from busyness by taking a light stretch. Please note, all yoga is not equal when it comes to preparing for sleep – the standing sequences are too enlivening! Opt instead for the calming floor-based routine from Step 2 (see page 69).

Comforting rituals

Soothe your nervous system with some self-massage. Try some of the options from Step 4 (see pages 111–20). Boost the relaxing properties of touch by adding magnesium oil spray for its anti-inflammatory effect. If it tingles on your limbs, try two sprays on each foot where the skin is less sensitive.

Breathwork

Combine breathing practices with scents you associate with relaxation and feel how it sets the scene for rest. Refer back to Step 4 (see page 127) for some ideas on practices.

Write it down

Organize your mind and lift your mood with a spot of pre-bedtime journalling. Save your "worry time" for a different period of the day and focus on the prompts that help you feel peaceful. You could plan your day ahead, helping you feel like you have the next day under control or, if you need something that diverts your attention from life's demands, close some tabs with a gratitude journalling practice (see page 181 for some reflective prompts based on gratitude).

Use technology mindfully

Seek out an app that can guide you to a place of serenity – meditation, relaxation, visualisation, yoga nidra, breathing... whatever resonates for you.

What to do when you can't sleep (or get back to sleep)

Even if you've taken in all of the earlier advice and tried a combination of different rituals, sometimes sleep just doesn't come (or stay). The key here is to make peace with wakefulness, occupying the mind with calming practices. How can we soften the mind and body into rest, reducing the pressure to sleep?

Try repeating a few mantras, cycling between:
"Just rest, sleep will come. Rest is just as good."
"I give myself permission to rest."
"I soften into this moment."

And if work or responsibilities tug at your attention:
"It's not time for that now, it's just time for me to flop and drop."
Try the "What got done" list in reverse (see page 189) or the "What went well and why".

You could also try imagined alternate nostril breathing (see page 124): don't use your hands to physically close off the nostrils, just imagine the flow in and out. And when all else fails, or if you're feeling agitated about being awake, get up and go somewhere else to do something soothing, until you feel sleepy again. Don't toss and turn for more than 20 minutes; it's better to get up and go back to your pre-bedtime routines to access a state of relaxation. Choose replenishing activities – this is not time for work or screens. There are two glorious restorative practices to enjoy later in this step – skip ahead at will!

Prime yourself for a
peaceful start to the day

The ease with which we greet the day starts with choices the night before. Make sure you give yourself enough time in bed to get the sleep you need. Streamline your mornings with preparations in advance, however you can simplify things. Make life easier for your future self by laying out clothes, packing your bag, planning your journey and knowing your go time. Consider a dawn-simulation lamp if the sound of your alarm sets your nervous system into "fight or flight" mode. What else can you do to make your mornings gentler? Creating a morning routine will help you greet the day with calm poise. Here's a simple one to work from.

Don't reach for your phone first thing: let worldly demands wait and instead tune inwards.

Meditate on the warmth and comfort of your bedding, enjoying the absence of doing.

Take a couple of relaxed breaths, feeling a sense of appreciation for a blank slate in front of you.

Gradually let the outer world in, listen for birds or the sounds of nature around you.

Before you leap into action, call to mind one thing you're looking forward to in your day (getting back into bed counts!)

Take 6 Mountain Breaths (see page 60) to uplift and energize yourself.

Get your rest on – you *are* thoroughly deserving of it

The benefits of rest, and why we need it even if we get decent sleep

- **Rest is for the wicked, right?** It couldn't be further from the truth. When we are well-rested we have greater access to kindness and compassion.
- **Rest is lazy, yes?** Think again. It's often easier to keep working and striving than it is to wrench ourselves away and switch off. If you've ever tried to develop a meditation, yoga, journaling or breathing practice – or even just attempted to get to bed at a reasonable time – you'll know the diligence and dedication this requires.
- **I sleep well so I don't need rest during the day?** Look at the number of choices you have to make in a day, the sheer volume of information you digest, the screen time, the sensory stimulation – one big recalibration overnight is insufficient. We need opportunities to reset over the course of our day so that we can function, let alone function well.

Of these benefits of rest, which ones speak to you?
There are so many advantages to rest, what will motivate you to claim the amount you deserve? The prompts later in this step on compassionate pace will hopefully give you the dispensation you're looking for.

- Improve your ability to learn and engage in complex thought.
- Increase your problem solving ability.
- Lift your mood.
- Stress relief.
- Nervous system regulation so you can stay calm and empathize.
- Productivity boost.
- Refresh your senses.
- Physical relaxation for tension and pain relief.
- Reduce inflammation and aid recovery and healing.
- Strengthen your immune system.
- Help you focus and remember.
- Break inertia and cultivate better decision-making power.
- Creativity boost.
- Protection from burnout.

When it comes to rest, nothing fancy is required. It can be as simple as curling up with the cat, snuggling in with a comforting read, gazing out of the window or zoning out with some calming music playing. You will know well the kind of restorative practices that speak to you, the key is to give yourself permission to engage in them.

For when you're exhausted, sleep-deprived or can't get to sleep[11]:
Three restorative practices to soothe

Legs Up The Wall

- Grab a selection of cushions, pillows, blankets, an eye mask if you have one and make sure you're wearing warm socks – this is the adult version of building a fort. We need either access to wall space, free of footfall and doors, or if you know you have tight hamstrings, you'll need to plonk yourself on the floor in front or your sofa or armchair.

- Begin by sitting on the floor, side on to the wall or base of the chair and roll onto your back, swinging your legs up the wall or onto the seat of the chair in front of you. Give the weight of your legs to the wall or chair and allow your whole body to drop.

- Maximize your comfort with a cushion or pillow beneath your head and wrap yourself warmly in blankets. Rest your eyes with an eye mask and set an alarm if you need to be up any time soon.

- Stay for 10 minutes or as long as your comfort and day allow. There is no pressure to drop off, just keep your mind tethered to something calming. Listen to music or a guided practice if your thoughts are tenacious or repeat one of your calming mantras.

- This pose is so healing because it redistributes the blood from your legs to your vital organs. Come out of the pose slowly, spending 10 breaths lying on your side with knees bent before gently coming up to sitting.

Savasana

- With the same selection of comforting props, this time you're going to arrange yourself so that you're lying on your back, legs and arms outstretched, with support for your head and beneath your knees so that your legs stay gently bent.

- Again, ensure your feet are warm, drape yourself in coverings and use your eye mask. Stay present to the sensations of your body relaxing or let yourself drop off.

- Do this for 5 minutes or as long as your day permits. *"Nothing to be done and nowhere else to be. Just breathe."*

Lie back & receive

- Snuggle in somewhere comfy and listen to something soothing. Opt for relaxing music, nature sounds, a guided relaxation like 'yoga nidra', a sleep story or a calming audio book.

- Allow the sound to wash over you and your body to receive the relaxation it delivers.

Micro Rest

Let's be honest, curling up for a snooze is often out of reach. Micro rest is an alternative if longer practices are inaccessible.

For when you'd like to nap but can't:
Three micro-practices

Massage your horns

- Release your face with this ritual, in particular the furrowed brow we make when we steel ourselves against the cold.

- Make a gentle fist with your hands, place the soft part of the base of your thumbs on your forehead where you would have two imaginary goaty horns. It doesn't have to be precise – just firmly press the base of your thumbs into your forehead where it feels good to you and observe how this releases your eyes and jaw, and slows down your breathing.

- Give yourself at least 10 calming breaths to reboot.

Get out your chicken wings

- Place your fingertips on your shoulders, forming "wings".

- As you inhale, slide your elbows forwards and up, then, as you exhale, circle them back and down.

- Repeat 10 times, feeling how this frees the chest and shoulders – breaking free of the winter slump and noticing how more alert you feel after just a few spacious breaths.

Hand balm ritual

- Get the oxytocin going by massaging in some hand balm with a scent that uplifts you. A simple energy boost!

Obstacles to rest

The pace of life can be so frenetic at times that we often feel like we don't have the time or space to rest; there's always something on else on the "to do" list. Now we've already debunked the myth that rest has to involve a significant investment of time, but you might feel a barrier to even the micro-moments of rest, feeling guilty for so much as a momentary pause. If this strikes a chord for you, I invite you to have a think about where these feelings come from, and ask yourself – are they true and do they serve you?

If you still feel an invisible barrier to rest, then bypass the roadblock and call it something else. The word "rest" has become laden with so much toxic baggage, so see how it feels to call it "rejuvenation" or "recharging"? Your mantra here is:

> *"My depletion serves no one and my replenishment serves everyone."*

Central to thriving in winter is cultivating a compassionate pace. Here are some other mantras and prompts to help you shift gears and better manage your energy and time, and a clarification on the meaning of each one:

> *"My capacity is not the same thing as my capability."*
>
> *I may be capable of this request, but do I have the capacity for it right now?*

> *"I give myself permission to choose."*
>
> *I recognize that not only do I have a choice, I give myself permission to choose.*

"In saying yes to this request, what does this mean I am saying no to?"

What are the costs of saying yes here in terms of time, energy and other resources? What else will be sacrificed to deliver this request?

"My free time is not my availability."

My down-time matters and it's ok to protect it.

"There are diminishing returns for pushing on."

Recognize when it's time to down tools. Yes, I could push on, but this may result in making errors, decision-making fatigue, slowed reaction time and less creativity.

"Taking a break isn't a distraction, it's an opportunity to recharge."

I fuel my car, reboot my computer and recharge my phone – I can also respect and lovingly tend to my own "energy bank".

Develop a Compassionate Pace: Sleep & Rest

REFLECTION TIME ON SLEEP & REST

What does rest facilitate in your life?

What brings you energy, what activities do you find restorative? How can you make space for them?

What do you find depleting? What can you minimize, avoid or do to compensate for these?

How will you allow yourself to slow down this winter? How will you keep an eye on sedentary periods, honouring your needs for both rest and movement?

Are there any lifestyle or environmental adjustments you can make to promote sleep? Are your pre-bedtime and morning routines working for you?

How is your rest routine serving you? Are there any commitments you'd like to make to yourself?

How will you pace yourself compassionately this winter?

6:
Make Meaningful Connections

Humans need social connection to thrive just as much as we need food and water. So how can we honour the impulse to retreat in winter without cutting ourselves off and laying ourselves vulnerable to loneliness? This chapter explores how to nurture a feeling of connection with those near to you, deepening your sense of belonging with them – regardless of proximity – and how to feel more connected with yourself. Loneliness is not just about a desire for connection, it is also acknowledging a need to feel understood. You will find practical suggestions on how to cultivate a sense of validation and belonging to something greater than ourselves, even in hibernation mode.

One of the greatest challenges of winter for many people is the sense of loneliness and isolation they feel. The desire to hunker down can mean we make fewer plans and social engagements can become few and far between. Fewer people out and about can mean there are reduced incidental opportunities for connection. Treacherous travelling conditions can be off-putting and inclement weather can make plans difficult to honour. Our social stamina might feel like it's gone out of the window. Low mood can wreak havoc with mental clarity and it can feel hard to muster the energy to reach out and connect. Maybe we feel like we're not much company and this adds to our feelings of alienation, creating a vicious cycle of further retreat and diminished mood. Winter can also be especially tough for those living on their own.

Just as we know we need to move our bodies for our mood, we need to plug in and share the journey with other human beings for our health. Loneliness has serious implications for our well-being, with our degree of social connectedness being linked with our quality of life and longevity. Extensive research demonstrates the importance of social relationships for promoting mental health and protecting ourselves from the development and progression of physical illness and disease[1]. How we connect might need some massaging over the winter months for it to feel both appealing and do-able. This is not just about nourishing our relationships with other people, it's also about nurturing our relationship with ourselves. Arguably, winter is an ideal opportunity for both.

How can we maximize harmony among our hibernating housemates?

Remember that winter can have a potent impact on mood and energy levels and this can have a knock-on effect in our relationships. When we're at a low ebb, it is harder to be the best version of ourselves. The key here is to be patient and compassionate, and to give each other – and ourselves – grace.

Try not to take other people's bad moods personally. Instead of muttering, "What's wrong with you?", consider the question: "What's happened to you?" It can help our stress levels and the health of our relationships to generate more charitable attributions to the behaviour of others. Rather than judgement and character assassination, reflecting on the genuine challenges we each face can have us rubbing along with less friction. It can be quite a gift to be allowed the space to express irritation, frustration, grief and sadness.

An important part of honouring our boundaries is giving feedback on how people around us are behaving, but don't let this dominate conversation. For our relationships to flourish, we need a ratio of 5:1 positive-to-negative interactions[2], so become skilled in the art of voicing appreciation. Let your nearest and dearest know what they've done well, thank them for their contributions and express your gratitude for the things you love about them.

It helps to become swift with our apologies too, remembering that a good apology includes a sincere communication of regret for harm caused and a commitment to avoiding the same error in future.

Rituals to reunite after a day apart can feed our relationships too. A simple way to stay current and facilitate reconnection is to ask in advance about events occurring in the day ahead so you have something to check in on when you next come together. Remembering these events not only gives us something to talk about, it is a powerful way to stoke empathy and understanding, helping our loved ones feel cared for.

Practices to alleviate loneliness & feel connected with others

Here are some simple ways to nourish your relationships and to help you plug in.

To identify your support network:
Who's in your circle?

- Grab a blank sheet of paper and make a list of all the people in your circle. Think broadly: include family members, close friends, people you share common interests or pursuits with. Incidental connections count too – like the people you click with at the school gate, your favourite coffee shop, even the people you gravitate to at the checkouts. Jot down all the people who help keep your health and well-being on radar – your hairdresser, acupuncturist, physio, dentist, coach... everyone who cares about and for you, everyone you care about, from the present moment to people you haven't spoken to for a decade.

- Look at this mind map of loving connection to remember the breadth of your circle.

To stay current & communicate care:
Express your thanks

- Spend some time reflecting on your mind map of people and if it resonates for you, jot down next to each name what you appreciate about them.

- Take this one step further and reach out to them, letting them know how much you value them and how they enrich your life. Send a hand-written letter, pick up the phone or just send a text of gratitude to the people who have made and continue to make a difference in your life. Let them know what they mean to you, how they make you feel, what you're thankful to them for.

- Feel how this not only lifts your collective spirits in the moment, but it also deepens your bonds.

To keep social connection a priority:
Spend time with your favourite people

- Reach out and make plans to build new memories, whether that's by coming together if you're in the same neck of the woods or making time and space to connect via the phone if you're far apart. It doesn't need to be anything grand or elaborate to plug in and feel connected.

- Give yourself permission to allow the shape of your social interactions to change with the seasons. The logistics of getting together in winter might be tricky, but seek common ground. It's ok to stay in for the evening and, let's be honest, anything past sundown can feel like a stretch. Instead, make plans for a walk and talk; winter can be the perfect time for coffee and brunch meet-ups.

To broaden your understanding of connection:
Reflect on different types of intimacy

- There are many ways that we can connect with other human beings and feel less alone. It might be interesting to consider how different relationships feed us in a variety of ways. Part of this comes down to the type of intimacy that we share with this other person. It also reminds us that our relationships don't have to meet all our needs; we can turn to different people to enjoy different forms of connection and self-expression.

Physical intimacy is about touch and closeness between bodies; it includes being inside someone's personal space, holding hands, cuddling, kissing or sex. Having a massage can satisfy our needs for physical intimacy, as can a hug with a friend or time spent with your pet. It's important to note, it's not just people who provide a deep sense of connection. Our pets can provide a powerful buffer from anxiety and depression too.[3]

Emotional intimacy is the closeness that comes from feeling safe and secure with another person, encompassing the feeling of being seen, known and understood. It involves getting to know each other deeply and can take some time to build.

Intellectual intimacy is the closeness that comes from sharing ideas and mind-stretching experiences. It comes from engaging in enriching conversation and the mental challenge of learning and growing together. It is about sharing ideas and thoughts even when we have differing opinions.

Spiritual intimacy is the closeness we feel when we connect with another person over shared world views, values and beliefs. It's the connection we feel when there is a sense of shared purpose and meaning.

- Return to your mind map of connections and consider who in your current circle you can connect with for these various forms of intimacy.

- How can you find ways to meet your needs for intimacy of the mind, heart, body and soul? Who might you reach out to? Are you open to welcoming new people into your circle and how might you go about that?

- Be gentle with yourself in this reflection and action planning.

The Science of hugs*

We learned about the hormone oxytocin in our previous step on the comforting properties of touch (see page 110). For the same reason, hugs are a beautiful way to create a feel-good hit.

There are so many different ways that hugs benefit us. They have the potential to boost your heart health[4] by lowering your blood pressure. They release oxytocin, which improves your relationships[5] and deepens your connection by enhancing a feeling of trust and support, reducing feelings of loneliness.

They are a beautiful wordless way to communicate care and understanding. By sending cues of safety to your nervous system they boost your stress tolerance and reduce anxiety[6]. During hugs, our bodies release serotonin and dopamine, making us feel happier[7].

Hugs can also alleviate pain[8], reduce signs of illness[9] and protect you from future ailments[10]. And you don't just benefit from receiving a hug, you benefit from giving one[11].

What makes a good hug? For hugs to be maximally effective they need to be mutually desired, they're best with the intent to express care, with a feeling of medium pressure and of a duration that you're all happy to be hugging[12].

*If you're on your own, feel free to flip back to Step 4 (see page 104) and seek out your favourite rituals of self-soothing. Research shows that snuggling with our pets counts and even hugging an inanimate object like a teddy bear can provide us with valuable support.

How to feel connected even when you're alone

There's a significant difference between solitude and feeling lonely. We just need strategies to help us craft a feeling of joy and contentment in time alone. How can we plug into a feeling of belonging even when we are on our own? The solution here is two-fold. We benefit from connecting with other people and by also coming home to ourselves. Time alone is a powerful opportunity to get to know ourselves better: our own feelings, needs, interests, preferences, desires and hopes[13].

Call to mind your social support.
Did you notice while making your mind map of loving connections a sense of warm feelings? (Look back at who's in your circle mind map on page 166.) Just recalling the people on our team and remembering their caring presence can help us feel better in the moment[14]. Imagining your loved ones helps to dial down loneliness and enhances a feeling of social connectedness[15]. We might be alone but we're not on our own. Spend some time thinking about the people who are there for you and remember the love goes on.

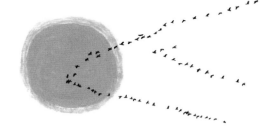

Get nostalgic

Take the previous practice one step further and recall a specific time when you felt connected with your loved ones. Relive it with all your senses and feel how it brings all those pleasant feelings flooding back, alleviating loneliness[16]. You can reminisce alone or you can share the experience with them by sending a little love note of "Remember when...". Even when our loved ones have passed, we can still feel connected by these loving memories, feeling anchored in that continued relationship.

Take an awe walk

It's not just connection with people we know that nourishes us, it's in moments of shared humanity with complete strangers, it's in connecting with Nature and feeling part of something bigger than ourselves. Be prepared that awe comes from many sources of different shapes and sizes. I remember one particularly bleak wet day where I'd gone out for my awe walk. I was nearly home, drenched from head to toe and was feeling disheartened that I hadn't yet found my awe experience, when this dear old lady huddled under a bus shelter sung out to me cheerily: "Careful, you might get wet!" Be open, awe will find you and it will fill you right back up. (For more details about this ritual, see page 92).

Find your tribe.

Connecting with like-minded people via communities or resources or finding other people who help you feel understood are powerful antidotes to loneliness. Seek out a sense of belonging by listening to podcasts on themes you care about and be an active part in the communities available online. You could listen to TED talks or radio programmes, watch films and TV shows, read Substack blogs, join an online book club, or volunteer for a charity that matters to you. Even reading a book with a protagonist who feels as you do can be validating. Think broadly and reach out to these sources of understanding and acceptance.

Connect with yourself

Last but not least, focus on your internal connection. Throughout this whole book have you felt the gentle invitation to come home to yourself? You've been reflecting on your thoughts and feelings from the very first page. Knowing yourself is one of the most powerful ways to move from feeling lonely to enjoying time alone. We are going to dive much deeper into this journey to self-awareness in our step on reflection, but for now, let's enjoy a simple check in.

Your guided practice to come home to yourself

Find a place of comfort where you won't be disturbed and settle in.

Bring your hands to your heart and feel their warmth.

Bring your mind to the sensation of your hands on your heart, dialling down the noise from outside of you, allowing you to hear what's happening within.

Feel your body sitting in stillness, the grounding of your feet, sit bones, back and hands.

Become aware of your breathing as you relax into stillness, knowing that there is nothing to change or manipulate, you're just feeling the sensation of breathing.

Notice the presence of any emotions without judgement, get curious about them and allow them to be there. If it's hard to put these into words, consider whether they have shape, or colour to them.

Notice the thoughts that come to you. It is ok for the mind to think – that's your mind's job and it's not our job to silence it. We just let the thoughts come and we let them go, bringing our attention back to this experience of sitting in stillness, connecting with ourselves.

In this process of noticing, are you becoming aware of any needs?

Are you hungry, thirsty, tired, jittery, low or lonely?

Is there a prescription of winter ingredients that might help you in this moment?

Do you need some light or colour? A dose of Nature?

Do you need to move your body? Stretch? Some comfort or laughter?

Do you seek a feeling of belonging or understanding?

Do you need a rest or an early night?

Is there something on your "to do" list tapping you on your shoulder, an incompletion that it would be satisfying to sort?

Is there a value that needs expressing or something that needs to be said?

Take action, my friend. How can you meet this need?

Even the smallest act of nourishment can make a tangible difference. Remember, your needs matter. The world needs resourced people.

REFLECTION TIME ON
MEANINGFUL CONNECTIONS

*Of the tips for keeping home life harmonious,
what speaks to you?*

*Are there commitments you'd like to make and
share with your housemates?*

≈

*Which strategies for feeling connected with loved
ones resonate for you?*

*How will you reach out and nurture the health
of your relationships?*

≈

*When you're alone, how will you plug in and find
that sense of connection with self, others and
things that matter to you?*

Write down your toolkit for navigating loneliness.

7:
Practise Reflection

As the weather closes in, we have no option but to retreat, providing us with the ideal opportunity to take stock, digest experiences, connect with our values and make some gentle plans for winter, the rebirth of spring and beyond. For some people, this comes naturally, but for others, this is a skill that takes some cultivation. If you're well-versed with your own reflective practices, grab your blank paper and pens and go for it, but if you need a little more direction, I have you covered in this step. Each winter that you revisit this book, you might find a different prompt or practice to explore. Approach with curiosity and be guided by what calls to you. There is no right or wrong.

Prompts to take stock

- What's happened in my year?
- My favourite memory was...
- What simple pleasures have I savoured?
- When did I feel at peace this year?
- When did I feel alive this year?
- When have I felt present?
- What aspects of my health do I feel grateful for?
- Who are my cheerleaders?
- What kindness have I received this year?
- What kindness have I extended to others this year?
- What's inspired me in this past year?
- Was there a time that I was brave this year?
- Reflecting on my relationship with myself, is it how I'd like it to be?

Prompts to digest your experiences

- What were my biggest challenges this year?
- What have been the high points?
- What was one small error I made this year? What would I say to a friend who confessed the same? How might I do things differently next time?
- What am I learning?
- How am I growing?
- I can be proud of...
- One barrier or obstacle I overcame was...
- One thing I achieved or succeeded in was...
- I am ready to let go of...

Prompts to connect you with your values

- What matters to me right now?
- What values do I want to weave into my life?
- What decisions or commitments am I proud of making?
- Which qualities make me feel alive and at peace?
- I am grateful for...
- I'm happy I made time for...
- I need less of...
- Was there a time when I felt impinged upon? What value was being compromised?
- What deserves to be celebrated?
- What deserves to be grieved?

Action planning prompts

- Winter is an opportunity for me to...
- What's important moving forwards?
- Is there an apology I need to make?
- Who has made a positive impact on me and have I expressed my appreciation?
- Is there someone I need to check in with and communicate care for?
- How can I connect with a sense of community?
- What incompletions do I need to take care of? Is there something I've been neglecting or putting off?
- Is there a boundary I need to adjust?
- If I wasn't concerned with other people's opinions of me, I would...
- How can I help keep promises to myself moving forwards?
- Are there any healthy habits I've forgotten about or that I want to reclaim?
- What nourishing activities do I need to make space for?
- Coming back to my relationship with me – how can I make it how I would like it to be? What would this facilitate in my life? What are the barriers and how can I overcome them?
- How can I show myself tenderness?
- How can I show myself respect?
- How can I be more caring towards myself?

Reflective practices to help you manage your mind, stress & emotions

To help you heal:
Write a compassionate letter to yourself

- When writing your letter, think about what you have been through recently or historically. How would anyone else feel had they had these same experiences? What would you say to someone you care about in the same circumstance? What do you want to say to yourself, or are there any words that you need to hear? Can you extend them to yourself now?

To help you let go:
Write a letter to someone who has treated you unfairly

- There is no intention to send this letter. Just jot down what happened from your perspective, how it made you feel and the impact it had on you. If you wish to express forgiveness, you are welcome to, but you don't need to. This is not about freeing the other person, it is helping you move through your feelings and say what you need to say, even though the letter is never delivered.

- Destroy the letter and give yourself permission to release with it whatever you are ready to let go, allowing it to be a gradual process.

To help you deal with self-criticism:
Counter your negative thoughts

- Call to mind one recurring negative thought that niggles at your self-esteem. Then jot down a couple of statements to counter this thought.

- If this is hard, what would you say to a loved one experiencing this thought? Is there a comforting ritual that could help you extend a little encouragement to yourself right now?

To boost your self-compassion:
Try a self-talk experiment

- Start with just noticing what you tell yourself and recognizing the impact it has on your mood, energy and confidence. Would you say it out loud? Would you say it to a stranger? Would you say it to someone dear to you?

- Once you've built your skills of noticing, get curious – tap into your sense of humour and reframe it into something more constructive, making sure it's fitting for a friend.

- Remember, no one is immune from crappy inner dialogue, just don't let it push you around. Give your brain something more constructive to anchor on and make sure you're not hungry or dehydrated. Sometimes we don't need another coping tool, we just need a hug or a break!

To boost your self-esteem:
Reflect on a recent challenge

- Identify the strengths or qualities that you drew upon to make it through this challenge. Is there a current difficulty in which you could again put this strength to good use?

- Remember, you don't have to face it alone. Is there someone you can reach out to for support?

To navigate anxiety:
Set aside some "worry time"

- We need to get really granular with this practice so it doesn't leak out and consume us. Schedule it in, avoiding the time right before bed, set a defined time limit (30 minutes max), think about where you will do it and consider how you will do it. Don't let "worry time" spiral into a negative thought loop.

- Try spending equal time generating the worst, best and most likely case scenarios and do some problem solving in response to catastrophic thoughts or undesired outcomes.

- Identify strategies that can overcome potential barriers and remember to stay anchored in what you have control over.

- Enlist a friend if you need support or a brainstorming partner.

To help you feel aligned:
Use a mantra to set an intention for the day

- Reflecting on what's to come, think of a quality that would help you navigate what's required of you to achieve what you want to today. It could be a single word, such as patience, creativity or courage.

- Repeat it at regular intervals, like whenever you check your inbox or take a sip of your water, and let it bring your values to everyday life.

To free up energy:
"Close some tabs"

- What unfinished business is weighing you down? Is there anything you need to sort out or resolve?

- Where will you take action? Think about: health, finances, career/work, house admin, car admin, social arrangements, inbox, corresepondence and your social media feed.

- Notice how you feel after you see these things through to completion.

To help you pace yourself:
Learn from previous experiences of depletion

- To be able to pace yourself, it helps to become aware of your early warning signs of stress or overwhelm. These states can show up in a variety of ways including the nature and quality of your thinking, in physical aches, pains and tension, feeling teary or reactive, and it can manifest in your behaviour too: for example, compulsive phone-scrolling. By identifying your signs and symptoms, you are better placed to take early nurturing action.

- If you feel guilty about taking a purposeful pause, it's worth reflecting on what happened in the past when you pushed through. Proactively plan what you will do differently the next time you feel your stress levels rising.

- If you're constantly treating your life like it's a checklist, think about how you can decide on your own milestones and measures of success.

- Think of rest and replenishment as the necessary fuel to do what's required of you, rather than the reward.

To feel at peace:
Recognize your accomplishments

- It is so easy to become fixated on all the things yet to be tackled and, given that life keeps happening, there's never a time when "everything is done". Take comfort in recognizing what we have managed to achieve.

- To bring a sense of accomplishment, identify three things that went well in your day, but don't stop there – ask yourself why that thing happened. Recognize the hand you played in it, the kindness you received or the good in the world that was behind this thing that you are grateful for. It's this part of the exercise that really lifts your mood.

- On days when "good things" feel sparse, make peace with it. We all have days like this. Instead of wracking your brain on what to feel grateful for, put together either mentally or on paper a quick list of "what got done". From the miniature to the mega, give a nod to it all. Recognize your effort, whether it was crossed off your list or not, and give yourself a pat on the back for the plethora of things you worked on. Start at the morning or go in reverse for a more soporific effect when your head hits the pillow. Well done, you.

REFLECTION TIME ON
YOUR OWN REFLECTIONS

This step is already jampacked with opportunities to reflect so, in closing, I invite you to make a note of the prompts or practices that speak to you; think about where you might do them and when it might work best for you.

Take note of your observations and see the fruits of your labour emerge!

Bringing All the Steps Together

Thank you for sharing this journey through winter with me. We have covered so much territory together, with a huge variety of nourishing practices to try and tips to integrate into everyday life. I hope that my 'out-of-towner' enthusiasm for winter has piqued your curiosity to the joy available to you this season, too. I hope you feel that you not only have fresh eyes and a sense of quiet hope, but a robust set of tools that will keep you even-keeled through the challenges we face in winter.

So how do you feel about this winter? How will you prepare or pace yourself throughout it? I hope this will be a book you return to on a yearly basis, like coming back to an old friend who will keep you company through the winter months, inviting you to slow down, check in and take good care of yourself.

On each read, I invite you to use the three Cs to bring together your thoughts and plans for this winter:

Curiosity – allow yourself to get curious about what this winter holds for you. Given the events unfolding in your life at the moment, the conditions where you are based, what feels like a resonant purpose for this winter? Given your health, your responsibilities, your available resources, what would you like this winter to be about? Is there a thread that feels uplifting, encouraging or motivating to you? Perhaps it's growth or healing. Maybe it's getting to know yourself. Could it be alignment, playfulness or hope? It could be going gently.

It might even be just getting through it. Sometimes survival mode is more than enough. Keep it light and do-able – we are in hibernation mode, after all – and we just need something to keep us anchored until the resurgence of energy that comes with spring. Remember, it is coming!

Compassion – life is constantly tugging at our attention. It's easy to get distracted by what other people are doing, or comparing yourself to what you've done in the past. Stay true to your purpose and write down what you give yourself permission to do this winter. Know that you are thoroughly deserving of all the nourishment, all the rejuvenation, all the winter joy, all the awe and all the compassionate pace.

Care – you've read about many different ways to keep feeling energized and clear-headed over winter, let's get clear now on the actions that feel most helpful in meeting your chosen purpose. The 7 Steps at a glance will give you a clue to the nourishment you need to thrive in winter and the steps are deliberately list-based and bite-sized so you can flick back through and pick your priorities with ease. Highlight the ones that feel inspiring to you for convenient reference or jot them down to keep these commitments fresh in your mind.

Remember
My purpose this winter....
I give myself permission to...
My priorities are...

Wishing you a delicious winter of your choosing!

Your Self-care Toolkit for Common Winter Ailments

Common Cold

There is no cure for the common cold, but there are remedies that can provide relief.

- Keep well hydrated.
- Keep warm.
- Get lots of rest and sleep.
- To soothe a sore throat, see the toolkit on page 199.
- Warm liquids can provide comfort.
- Use saline drops or sprays to relieve congestion.
- Over-the-counter medications such as paracetamol or ibuprofen can help manage pain.
- Cold and flu medications (not to be combined with other over-the-counter pain medication) can relieve symptoms of congestion, but don't be fooled into thinking this expedites healing – they just mask the symptoms, so don't overdo it.
- Ginger, honey and garlic have antimicrobial properties that may help recovery.
- Topical ointments with camphor, tea tree, eucalyptus and menthol can help relieve congestion.
- Wash your hands frequently.

Flu

How do you tell the difference between a common cold and flu? While they have similar symptoms, flu tends to be more severe.

Cold	Flu
Gradual onset	Appears rapidly, onset of a few hours
Affects primarily the throat	Affects more than just the nose and throat
Makes you feel unwell, but you feel ok to carry on with normal responsibilities	Makes you feel exhausted and unable to meet the usual demands of your day

Symptoms of the flu include a sudden high temperature, aching body, sore throat, blocked nose, dry cough, headache, exhaustion, difficulty sleeping, loss of appetite, diarrhoea, stomach pain, nausea and vomiting.

- Get as much rest and sleep as possible.
- Stay warm.
- Keep well hydrated.
- Take paracetamol or ibuprofen to manage pain.
- Wash your hands frequently to avoid spreading germs.

Cough

- Get plenty of rest.
- Stay well hydrated, taking regular sips can help.
- Take paracetamol or ibuprofen for pain relief.
- Hot lemon water or tea with honey can provide soothing (honey is not suitable for babies under one).
- Cough syrups can help.
- Avoid medicated lozenges with menthol and other substances that can dry out the throat further, opt for honey-based lozenges instead.
- Keep a log of cough triggers.
- If cold air is a trigger, wrap a scarf around your mouth when outdoors to filter the cold air and breathe through your nose.
- Try swallowing instead of coughing.
- As much as possible, use nasal breathing, which reduces dry air irritating the throat.
- Directing the breath into the abdomen can help – try "chin mudra" to support abdominal breathing. Bring your thumb and forefinger to touch and feels how this makes it easier to breathe into your tummy.
- Keep your home dust- and damp-free.
- Avoid caffeine and alcohol, which can dry the throat.
- Breathe in steam from a bowl of boiled water with a towel over your head. The humidified air can provide some relief.

Sore throat

- Keep well-hydrated.
- Get lots of rest and sleep.
- Gargle with warm, salty water.
- Add honey to tea or take a spoonful on its own (never give honey to babies under one year of age).
- Eat cool or soft foods.
- Avoid smoke and smoking.
- Avoid alcohol.
- Make sure there are plenty of antioxidants in your diet.
- Add garlic for its antimicrobial properties.
- Anti-inflammatory lozenges can help.
- Take ibuprofen or paracetamol for pain relief as needed.
- Wash your hands regularly.

Chapped hands

- Keep your hands dry and warm.
- Protect your hands with gloves while outdoors.
- Wash your hands with a gentle cleanser without perfume and use warm rather than hot water.
- Keep hand balm by your sink and routinely apply it after washing your hands, keep another by the front door and apply before leaving the house. Carry another tube with you and apply after hand sanitizer when out and about.
- Keep well-hydrated.
- Eat oily fish or take a fish oil supplement.
- Avoid using hot-air hand dryers.
- Be careful with hand sanitizers that dry the skin more than soap does.

Cracked lips

- Try not to lick, bite or pick your lips.
- Avoid using products that sting, irritate or dry your lips.
- Steer clear of lip products containing camphor, eucalyptus, fragrance, menthol, oxybenzone, phenol, salicylic acid and flavours including citrus, mint and peppermint.
- To promote healing, opt for products using ingredients such as hemp seed oil, castor oil, ceramides, shea butter, beeswax or white petroleum jelly.
- Apply balm several times daily; every two hours if outdoors.
- In cold, windy weather, consider covering your lips with a scarf for extra protection.
- Drink plenty of water and be careful with your alcohol intake.
- Include oily fish in your diet or take fish oil supplements.
- Get plenty of rest and sleep.
- Wash your hands before applying balms and don't share them to avoid spreading germs.

Chilblains

Chilblains are small, itchy, inflamed patches that appear on the skin caused by poor circulation when exposed to the cold. It mostly occurs on the fingers and toes but the small blister-like patches can also affect the face and legs. Symptoms occur a few hours after being in the cold and tend to resolve themselves.

- To reduce the likelihood of chilblains from appearing, wear protective clothing that keeps you both warm and dry, especially the extremities. Wear gloves and thick socks when in the cold or damp. Avoid tight-fitting garments, which can restrict circulation and make you more susceptible to chilblains.

Avoid placing your hands and feet near radiators or under hot water to heat them up because this can cause swelling. Warm them up gradually. Give caffeinated drinks a miss because these can affect blood flow to the fingers and toes.

- If chilblains appear, leave the skin alone. Take paracetamol or ibuprofen for pain relief.

Raynaud's

Raynaud's phenomenon is a condition where exposure to the cold stops blood flowing properly to fingers and toes, resulting in a sensation of coldness, numbness and a feeling of prickling and stinging as you warm them up again. People with Raynaud's need to take extra precautions to protect themselves from the cold.

- Avoid caffeine and alcohol.
- Make a commitment to regular exercise for its benefits to circulation.
- Omega-3 fatty acids and a diet rich in antioxidants can help reduce symptoms.
- Engage in practices to manage stress and anxiety – take your pick of the comforting strategies in Step 4 (see page 104).

Aches & pains

- Keep yourself warm both indoors and out with plenty of layers that you can adjust for comfort. Thermal under layers, insulated gloves, warm socks and waterproof footwear will help protect you from the cold and damp winter conditions that can exacerbate joint and muscular aches and pains.
- When choosing your fresh fruit and veg, eat a rainbow of colours to reap the antioxidants and have a regular dose of oily fish for its omega-3 fatty acids, both of which reduce inflammation. Avoid processed foods, which can contribute to flare-ups.
- Be mindful of your posture while sitting and standing – we can unwittingly add to tension by slouching or creating asymmetry in our posture.
- Keep moving your body to reduce stiffness and to maintain your strength, flexibility, mobility and bone health. It can be a fine balance to strike, so keeping a note of your movement and your symptoms might help you better pace yourself. If you're new to exercise or integrating new ways of moving, be careful not to overdo it. Slowly build up over time and remember that movement doesn't have to be done in one go, it can be a few minutes here and there spread out over the whole course of your day, guided by your comfort.
- Break up periods of prolonged sitting ideally every 30 minutes. You'll find plenty of gentle movement inspiration in the sequences in Step 2 (see page 56).

- Hydration is key – dehydration can increase sensitivity to aches and pains, reduce joint lubrication and lead to muscle cramps. Pay attention to meeting your hydration needs and avoid substances that lead to dehydration, such as caffeine and alcohol.
- Take a warm bath to soothe joints and muscles and add some magnesium flakes for their anti-inflammatory properties.
- Heating pads and weighted blankets can also provide pain relief.
- Over-the-counter medications can help manage symptoms.
- Reach out for social support to help you navigate the emotional effects of managing pain and extend all the tenderness to yourself using the comforting practices in Step 4 (see page 104).

Winter blues

- Make sure you get your daily dose of sunlight and get out in Nature.
- Move your body daily in ways that feel joyful. Remember that stretching counts on low energy days.
- Feed your brain and hydrate your mood.
- Keep cosy and warm.
- Reach out and stay connected.
- Seek professional support and talk it through.
- If you're low in vitamin B12, a B12 oral spray may give you an energy boost.
- Invest in rest and bring regularity to your sleep.
- Engage in practices that bring you a lift – like breathing, touch and self-massage.
- Use a dawn-simulation lamp for a kinder start to the day.
- Be mindful of alcohol.
- Speak to your GP about a care plan – you don't have to face this alone.
- Keep a diary to remind yourself, by plotting your actions and progress, that your feelings change.
- Remind yourself that this is a season and it won't be like this forever.
- Be gentle with yourself.

References

1   Young, Emma, "Seasons and the Psyche", The Psychologist, The British Psychological Society (31 October 2023, bps.org.uk/psychologist/seasons-and-psyche)

2   Dzogang, Fabon; Lightman, Stafford; Cristianini, Nello, "Circadian mood variations in Twitter content", Brain and Neuroscience Advances, vol. 1 (1 December 2017, doi.org/10.1177/2398212817744501)

3   Meyer, Christelle; Muto, Vincenzo; Jaspar, Mathieu; Kussé, Caroline; Lambot, Erik; Chellappa, Sarah L; Degueldre, Christian; Balteau, Evelyne; Luxen, André; Middleton, Benita; Archer, Simon N; Collette, Fabienne; Dijk, Derk-Jan; Phillips, Christophe; Maquet, Pierre; Vandewalle, Gilles, "Seasonality in human cognitive brain responses", PNAS, vol. 113, no. 11 (8 February 2016, doi.org/10.1073/pnas.1518129113)

4   Lim, Andrew SP; Gaiteri, Chris; Yu, Lei; Sohail, Shahmir; Swardfager, Walter; Tasaki, Shinya; Schneider, Julia A; Paquet, Claire; Stuss, Donald T; Masellis, Mario; Black, Sandra E; Hugon, Jaques; Buchman, Aron S; Barnes, Lisa L; Bennett, David A; De Jager, Philip L, "Seasonal plasticity of cognition and related biological measures in adults with and without Alzheimer disease: Analysis of multiple cohorts", PLoS Medicine, vol. 15, no. 9 (4 Sep 2018 doi.org/10.1371/journal.pmed.1002647)

5   Leibowitz, Kari; Vittersø, Joar, "Winter is coming: Wintertime mindset and wellbeing in Norway", The International Journal of Wellbeing, vol. 10, no. 4 (30 September 2020, doi.org/10.5502/ijw.v10i4.935)

6   Wehr, TA; Rosenthal, NE, "Seasonality and affective illness", The American Journal of Psychiatry, 146(7) (July 1989, doi.org/10.1176/ajp.146.7.829).

7   "Seasonal Affective Disorder", National Institute of Mental Health (nimh.nih.gov/health/publications/seasonal-affective-disorder)

8   De la Iglesia, Horacio O; Fernández-Duque, Eduardo; Golombek, Diego A; Lanza, Norberto; Duffy, Jeanne F; Czeisler, Charles A; Valeggia, Claudia R, "Access to Electric Light Is Associated with Shorter Sleep Duration in a Traditionally Hunter-Gatherer Community", Journal of Biological Rhythms, vol. 30, issue 4, (August 2015, doi.org/10.1177/0748730415590702)

9   Huang, Di; Taha, Maie S; Nocera, Angela L; Workman, Alan D; Amiji, Mansoor M; Bleier, Benjamin S, "Cold exposure impairs extracellular vesicle swarm–mediated nasal antiviral immunity", The Journal of Allergy and Clinical Immunology, vol. 151, issue 2 (February 2023, doi.org/10.1016/j.jaci.2022.09.037)

10   Phan, Thieu X; Jaruga, Barbara; Pingle, Sandeep C; Bandyopadhyay, Bidhan C; Ahern, Gerard P, "Intrinsic Photosensitivity Enhances Motility of T Lymphocytes", Scientific Reports, 6 (20 December 2016, doi.org/10.1038/srep39479)

11   Dantzer, Robert; Kelley, Keith W; "Twenty years of research on cytokine-induced sickness behavior", Brain, Behavior, and Immunity, vol 21, issue 2 (February 2007, doi.org/10.1016/j.bbi.2006.09.006)

12   Miller, Andrew H; Raison, Charles L, "The role of inflammation in depression: from evolutionary imperative to modern treatment target", Nature Reviews Immunology, vol. 16 (29 December 2015, doi.org/10.1038/nri.2015.5)

13   Capita, Rosa and Alonso-Calleja, "Differences in reported winter and summer dietary intakes in young adults in Spain", International Journal of Food Sciences and Nutrition, 56:6 (6 July 2009, doi.org/10.1080/09637480500407875)

14   Ma, Y; Olendzki, B; Li, W; et al, "Seasonal variation in food intake, physical activity, and body weight in a predominantly overweight population", European Journal of Clinical Nutrition, vol. 60 (7 December 2005, doi.org/10.1038/sj.ejcn.1602346)

15   Shephard, Roy J; Aoyagi, Yukitoshi; "Seasonal variations in physical activity and implications for human health", European Journal of Applied Physiology, vol. 107 (2009, doi.org/10.1007/s00421-009-1127-1)

16   Okada, Masahiro, "Influence of Muscle Mass and Outdoor Environmental Factors on Appetite and Satiety Feeling in Young Japanese Women", International Journal of Environmental Research and Public Health, 15(1) (21 January 2018, doi.org/10.3390/ijerph15010167)

17   Van Cappellen, Patty; Ladd, Kevin L; Cassidy, Stephanie; Edwards, Megan E; Fredrickson, Barbara L; "Bodily feedback: expansive and upward posture facilitates the experience of positive affect", Cognition and Emotion, vol. 36 (4 August 2022, 10.1080/02699931.2022.2106945)

18 Veenstra, Lotte; Schneider, Iris K; Koole, Sander L; "Embodied mood regulation: the impact of body posture on mood recovery, negative thoughts, and mood-congruent recall", Cognition and Emotion, vol. 31 (14 September 2016, doi.org/10.1080/02699931.2016.1225003)

19 Wilkes, Carissa; Kydd, Rob; Sagar, Mark; Broadbent, Elizabeth, "Upright posture improves affect and fatigue in people with depressive symptoms", Journal of Behavior Therapy and Experimental Psychiatry, vol. 54 (March 2017, doi.org/10.1016/j.jbtep.2016.07.015)

20 Wilson, Vietta E; Peper, Erik, "The Effects of Upright and Slumped Postures on the Recall of Positive and Negative Thoughts", Applied Psychophysiology and Biofeedback, 29 (3) (2004, doi.org/10.1023/B:APBI.0000039057.32963.34)

21 "Seasonal variations in electricity demand", gov.uk (assets.publishing.service.gov.uk/media/5a7ba36540f0b645ba3c59b2/Seasonal_variations_in_electricity_demand.pdf)

22 Berman, Marc G; Jonides, John; Kaplan, Stephen, "The Cognitive Benefits of Interacting With Nature", Psychological Science, vol. 19, issue 12 (2008, https://doi.org/10.1111/j.1467-9280.2008.02225.x)

23 Berman, Marc G; Kross, Ethan; Krpan, Katherine M; Askren, Mary K; Burson, Aleah; Deldin, Patricia J; Kaplan, Stephen; Sherdell, Lindsey; Gotlib, Ian H; Jonides, John,

    "Interacting with nature improves cognition and affect for individuals with depression," Journal of Affective Disorders, vol 140, issue 3 (2012, doi.org/10.1016/j.jad.2012.03.012)

24 Jimenez, Marcia P; DeVille, Nicole V; Elliott, Elise G; Schiff, Jessica E; Wilt, Grete E; Hart, Jaime E; James, Peter, "Associations between Nature Exposure and Health: A Review of the Evidence", International Journal of Environmental Research and Public Health, 18(9) (April 30 2021, doi.org/10.3390/ijerph18094790)

25 Timothy D. Wilson et al, "Just think: The challenges of the disengaged mind," Science, vol 345, issue 6192, (4 July 2014, science.org/doi/10.1126/science.1250830)

Step 1: Harness Light & Colour

1   Blume, Christine; Garbazza, Corrado; Spitschan, Manuel, "Effects of light on human circadian rhythms, sleep and mood", Somnologie, vol. 23 (August 2019, doi.org/10.1007/s11818-019-00215-x)

Step 3: Embrace Nature

1   Wacker, Matthias; Holick, Michael F, "Sunlight and Vitamin D", Dermato-Endocrinology, vol. 5, issue 1 (January 2013, doi.org/10.4161/derm.24494)

2   Raymond-Lezman, Jonathan R; Riskin, Suzanne I, "Benefits and Risks of Sun Exposure to Maintain Adequate Vitamin D Levels", Cureus, 15(5) (May 2023, pubmed.ncbi.nlm.nih.gov/37284402/)

3   Wang, Jie; Wei, Zhen; Yao, Nan; Li, Caifeng; Sun, Long, "Association Between Sunlight Exposure and Mental Health: Evidence from a Special Population Without Sunlight in Work", Risk Management and Healthcare Policy, vol. 16 (14 June 2023, doi.org/10.2147/RMHP.S420018)

4   Phan, Thieu X; Jaruga, Barbara; Pingle, Sandeep C; Bandyopadhyay, Bidhan C; Ahern, Gerard P, "Intrinsic Photosensitivity Enhances Motility of T Lymphocytes", Scientific Reports, 6 (20 December 2016, doi.org/10.1038/srep39479)

5   Hägerhäll, Caroline; Laike, Thorbjörn; Küller, M; Marcheschi, Elizabeth; Boydston, C; Taylor, Richard P, "Human Physiological Benefits of Viewing Nature: EEG Responses to Exact and Statistical Fractal Patterns", Nonlinear Dynamics, Psychology, and Life Sciences, vol. 19, no. 1 (January 2015, pubmed.ncbi.nlm.nih.gov/25575556/)

6   Zhang, YD; Fan, SJ; Zhang, Z; Li, JX; Liu, XX; Hu, LX; Knibbs, LD; Dadvand, P; Jalaludin, B; Browning, MHEM; Zhao, T; Heinrich, J; He, Z; Chen, CZ; Zhou, Y; Dong, GH; Yang, BY, "Association between Residential Greenness and Human Microbiota: Evidence from Multiple Countries", Environmental Health Perspectives, vol. 131, issue 8 (2023 August, doi.org/10.1289/EHP12186)

7   Lowry, CA; Hollis, JH; de Vries, A; Pan, B; Brunet, LR; Hunt, JRF; Paton, JFR; van Kampen, E; Knight, DM; Evans, AK; Rook, GAW; Lightman, SL, "Identification of an immune-responsive mesolimbocortical serotonergic system: Potential role in regulation of emotional behavior", Neuroscience, vol. 142, issue 2 (11 May 2007, doi.org/10.1016/j.neuroscience.2007.01.067)

8   Li, Q; Morimoto, K; Nakadai, A, et al. "Forest Bathing Enhances Human Natural Killer Activity and Expression of Anti-Cancer Proteins", International Journal of Immunopathology and Pharmacology, 20 (April 2007, doi.org/10.1177/03946320070200S2)

9   Xiao, S; Wei, T; Petersen, JD, et al, "Biological effects of negative air ions on human health and integrated multiomics to identify biomarkers: a literature review", Environmental Science and Pollution Research, vol. 30 (12 May, 2023, doi.org/10.1007/s11356-023-27133-8)

10 Ulrich, Roger S, "View Through a Window May Influence Recovery from Surgery", Science, vol. 224, issue 4647 (April 1984, science.org/doi/10.1126/science.6143402)

11 Martin, Leanne; Pahl, Sabine; White, Mathew P; May, Jon, "Natural environments and craving: The mediating role of negative affect", Health & Place, vol. 58 (July 2019, doi.org/10.1016/j.healthplace.2019.102160)

12 Barton, Jo; Pretty, Jules, "What is the Best Dose of Nature and Green Exercise for Improving Mental Health? A Multi-Study Analysis", Environmental Science & Technology, (2010, doi.org/10.1021/es903183r)

13 Park, Bum Jin; Tsunetsugu, Yuko; Kasetani, Tamami, et al, "The physiological effects of Shinrin-yoku (taking in the forest atmosphere or forest bathing): evidence from field experiments in 24 forests across Japan", Environmental Health and Preventative Medicine, vol. 15 (May 2009, doi.org/10.1007/s12199-009-0086-9)

14 Sudimac, Sonja; Sale, Vera; Kühn, Simone, "How nature nurtures: Amygdala activity decreases as the result of a one-hour walk in nature", Molecular Psychiatry, vol. 27 (5 September 2022, doi.org/10.1038/s41380-022-01720-6)

15 van den Berg, Agnes E; Maas, Jolanda; Verheij, Robert A; Groenewegen, Peter P, "Green space as a buffer between stressful life events and health", Social Science & Medicine, vol 70, issue 8 (April 2010, doi.org/10.1016/j.socscimed.2010.01.002)

16   Wapner, Jessica, "Vision and Breathing May Be the Secrets to Surviving 2020", Scientific American (16 November 2020, scientificamerican.com/article/vision-and-breathing-may-be-the-secrets-to-surviving-2020/)

17   Kexiu, L; Elsadek, M; Liu, B; Fujii, E, "Foliage colors improve relaxation and emotional status of university students from different countries", Heliyon, vol. 7, issue 1 (31 January 2021, doi.org/10.1016/j.heliyon.2021.e06131)

18   University of Exeter, "Why plants in the office make us more productive" (1 September 2014, news-archive.exeter.ac.uk/featurednews/title_409094_en.html)

19   Faber Taylor, Andrea; Kuo, Frances E, "Children With Attention Deficits Concentrate Better After Walk in the Park", Journal of Attention Disorders, vol. 12, issue (March 2009, doi.org/10.1177/1087054708323000)

20   Berto, Rita, "Exposure to restorative environments helps restore attentional capacity", Journal of Environmental Psychology, vol. 25, issue 3, (September 2005, doi.org/10.1016/j.jenvp.2005.07.001)

21   University of Michigan, "Going outside – even in the cold – improves memory, attention" (16 December 2008, news.umich.edu/going-outsideeven-in-the-coldimproves-memory-attention/)

22   Bratman, Gregory N; Hamilton, J Paul; Hahn, Kevin S; Gross, James J, "Nature experience reduces rumination and subgenual prefrontal cortex activation" PNAS (29 June 2015, doi.org/10.1073/pnas.1510459112)

23   Morita, E; Fukuda, S; Nagano, J; Hamajima, N; Yamamoto, H; Iwai, Y; Nakashima, T; Ohira, H; Shirakawa, T, "Psychological effects of forest environments on healthy adults: Shinrin-yoku (forest-air bathing, walking) as a possible method of stress reduction", Public Health, vol. 121, issue 1 (January 2007, doi.org/10.1016/j.puhe.2006.05.024)

24   Bowler, DE; Buyung-Ali, LM; Knight, TM, et al. "A systematic review of evidence for the added benefits to health of exposure to natural environments", BMC Public Health, vol. 10 (4 August 2010, doi.org/10.1186/1471-2458-10-456)

25 Hammoud, Ryan; Tognin, Stefania; Bakolis, Ioannis, et al, "Lonely in a crowd: investigating the association between overcrowding and loneliness using smartphone technologies", Scientific Reports, 11 (20 December 2021, doi. org/10.1038/s41598-021-03398-2)

26 Russell, Roly; Guerry, Anne D; Balvanera, Patricia; Gould, Rachelle K; Basurto, Xavier; Chan, Kai MA; Klain, Sarah; Levine, Jordan; Tam, Jordan, "Humans and Nature: How Knowing and Experiencing Nature Affect Well-Being" Annual Review of Environment and Resources, vol. 38 (2 August 2013, doi.org/10.1146/annurev-environ-012312-110838)

27 Sturm, Virginia E; Datta, Samir; Roy, Ashlin RK; Sible, Isabel J; Kosik, Eena L; Veziris, Christina R; Chow, Tiffany E; Morris, Nathaniel A; Neuhaus, John; Kramer, Joel H; Miller, Bruce L; Holley, Sarah R; Keltner, Dacher, "Big smile, small self: Awe walks promote prosocial positive emotions in older adults", Emotion, 22(5) (2022, doi. org/10.1037/emo0000876)

28 Allen, Summer, "The Science of Awe", Greater Good Science Center at UC Berkeley (September 2018, ggsc.berkeley.edu/images/uploads/GGSC-JTF_ White_Paper-Awe_FINAL.pdf)

29 Ryan, Richard M; Weinstein, Netta; Bernstein, Jessey; Brown, Kirk Warren; Mistretta, Louis; Gagné, Marylène, "Vitalizing effects of being outdoors and in nature", Journal of Environmental Psychology, vol. 30, issue 2 (June 2010, doi. org/10.1016/j.jenvp.2009.10.009)

30 Piper, Emily, "Towards Healing Ambiguous Grief with Nature-Based Expressive Arts Therapy, Embodiment, and Mindfulness: A Literature Review", Expressive Therapies Capstone Theses (15 April 2019, digitalcommons.lesley.edu/ expressive_theses/166)

31 Cameron-Faulkner, Thea; Melville, Joanna; Gattis, Merideth, "Responding to nature: Natural environments improve parent-child communication", Journal of Environmental Psychology, vol 59 (October 2018, doi.org/10.1016/j. jenvp.2018.08.008)

32 Weinstein, Netta; Przybylski, Andrew K; Ryan, Richard M, "Can Nature Make Us More Caring? Effects of Immersion in Nature on Intrinsic Aspirations and Generosity", Personality and Social Psychology Bulletin, vol. 35, issue 10 (5 August, 2009, doi.org/10.1177/0146167209341649)

33 Masters, Alina; Pandi-Perumal, Seithikurippu R, Seixas, Azizi; Girardin, Jean-Louis; McFarlane, Samy I, "Melatonin, the Hormone of Darkness: From Sleep Promotion to Ebola Treatment", Brain Disorders and Therapy, 4(1), (2014, ncbi.nlm.nih.gov/pmc/articles/PMC4334454/)

34 Wainwright, Alfred, A Coast to Coast Walk (Frances Lincoln; 2017)

Step 4: Savour Comforting Rituals

1 Lejeune, MP; Westerterp, KR; Adam, TC; Luscombe-Marsh, ND; Westerterp-Plantenga, MS, "Ghrelin and glucagon-like peptide 1 concentrations, 24-h satiety, and energy and substrate metabolism during a high-protein diet and measured in a respiration chamber", The American Journal of Clinical Nutrition, vol. 83, issue 1, (January 2006, doi.org/10.1093/ajcn/83.1.89)

2 Janssens, PL; Hursel, R; Westerterp-Plantenga, MS, "Capsaicin increases sensation of fullness in energy balance, and decreases desire to eat after dinner in negative energy balance", Appetite, vol. 77 (June 2014, doi.org/10.1016/j.appet.2014.02.018)

3 Jach, ME; Serefko, A; Szopa, A; Sajnaga, E; Golczyk, H; Santos, LS; Borowicz-Reutt, K; Sieniawska, E, "The Role of Probiotics and Their Metabolites in the Treatment of Depression", Molecules, 28(7) (4 April 2023, doi.org/10.3390/molecules28073213)

4 Hoepner, CT; McIntyre, RS; Papakostas, GI, "Impact of Supplementation and Nutritional Interventions on Pathogenic Processes of Mood Disorders: A Review of the Evidence", Nutrients (26 February 2021, doi.org/10.3390/nu13030767)

5 Sarris, J; Ravindran, A; Yatham, LN; Marx, W; Rucklidge, JJ; McIntyre, RS; Akhondzadeh, S; Benedetti, F; Caneo, C; Cramer, H; Cribb, L,' de Manincor, M; Dean, O; Deslandes, AC; Freeman, MP; Gangadhar, B; Harvey, BH; Kasper, S; Lake, J; Lopresti, A; Lu, L; Metri, NJ; Mischoulon, D; Ng, CH; Nishi, D; Rahimi, R; Seedat, S; Sinclair, J; Su, KP; Zhang, ZJ; Berk, M, "Clinician guidelines for the treatment of psychiatric disorders with nutraceuticals and phytoceuticals: The World Federation of Societies of Biological Psychiatry (WFSBP) and Canadian Network for Mood and Anxiety Treatments (CANMAT) Taskforce", The World Journal of Biological Psychiatry, vol. 23, issue 6 (March 2022, doi.org/10.1080/15622975.2021.2013041)

6   Uvnäs-Moberg, Kerstin; Handlin, Linda; Petersson, Maria, "Self-soothing behaviors with particular reference to oxytocin release induced by non-noxious sensory stimulation", Frontiers in Psychology, vol 5 (12 January 2015, doi.org/10.3389/fpsyg.2014.01529)

7   Heatley Tejada, A; Dunbar, RIM; & Montero, M, "Physical Contact and Loneliness: Being Touched Reduces Perceptions of Loneliness", Adaptive Human Behavior and Physiology, vol. 6 (26 May 2020, doi.org/10.1007/s40750-020-00138-0)

8   Baumgartner, Jennifer N; Quintana, Desiree; Leija, Linda; Schuster, Nathaniel M; Bruno, Kelly A; Castellanos, Joel P; Case, Laura K, "Widespread Pressure Delivered by a Weighted Blanket Reduces Chronic Pain: A Randomized Controlled Trial", The Journal of Pain, vol. 23, issue 1 (January 2022, doi.org/10.1016/j.jpain.2021.07.009)

9   Vinson Jaime; Powers, Jan; Mosesso, Kelly, "Weighted Blankets: Anxiety Reduction in Adult Patients Receiving Chemotherapy", Clinical Journal of Oncology Nursing, no. 4 (1 August 2020, pubmed.ncbi.nlm.nih.gov/32678376)

10 Ekholm, Bodil; Spulber, Stefan; Adler, Mats, "A randomized controlled study of weighted chain blankets for insomnia in psychiatric disorders", Journal of Clinical Sleep Medicine, (15 September 2020, doi.org/10.5664/jcsm.8636)

11 Telles, S; Nagarathna, R; Nagendra, HR, "Breathing through a particular nostril can alter metabolism and autonomic activities", Indian Journal of Physiology and Pharmacology, 38(2): (April 1994, pubmed.ncbi.nlm.nih.gov/8063359/)

12 Pal, Gopal K; Agarwal, Ankit; Karthik, Shanmugavel; Pal, Pravati; Nanda, Nivedita, "Slow yogic breathing through right and left nostril influences sympathovagal balance, heart rate variability, and cardiovascular risks in young adults", North American Journal of Medical Sciences, 6(3) (March 2014, ncbi.nlm.nih.gov/pmc/articles/PMC3978938/)

13 Gov.uk, "Understanding and addressing the health risks of damp and mould in the home" (7 September 2023, gov.uk/government/publications/damp-and-mould-understanding-and-addressing-the-health-risks-for-rented-housing-providers/understanding-and-addressing-the-health-risks-of-damp-and-mould-in-the-home—2)

Step 5: Develop a Compassionate Pace: Sleep & Rest

1   Eanes, Linda, "CE: Too Much Sitting: A Newly Recognized Health Risk", American Journal of Nursing, 118(9) (September 2018; pubmed.ncbi.nlm.nih.gov/30113925/)

2   Seidler, Aileen; Weihrich, Katy Sarah; Bes, Frederik; de Zeeuw, Jan; Kunz, Dieter, "Seasonality of human sleep: Polysomnographic data of a neuropsychiatric sleep clinic", Frontiers in Neuroscience, vol. 17 (17 February 2023, doi.org/10.3389/fnins.2023.1105233)

3   Watson, NF; Badr, MS; Belenky, G; Bliwise, DL; Buxton, OM; Buysse, D; Dinges, DF; Gangwisch, J; Grandner, MA; Kushida, C; Malhotra, RK; Martin, JL; Patel, SR; Quan, SF; Tasali, E, "Recommended Amount of Sleep for a Healthy Adult: A Joint Consensus Statement of the American Academy of Sleep Medicine and Sleep Research Society", Sleep, vol. 38, issue 6 (1 June 2015, doi.org/10.5665/sleep.4716)

4   Hirshkowitz, M; Whiton, K; Albert, SM; Alessi, C; Bruni, O, et al, "The National Sleep Foundation's sleep time duration recommendations: methodology and results summary", Sleep Health, vol.1, issue 1 (March 2015, doi.org/10.1016/j.sleh.2014.12.010)

5   Murphy Patricia J; Campbell Scott S, "Nighttime drop in body temperature: a physiological trigger for sleep onset?" Sleep, vol. 20, issue 7 (July 1997, doi.org/10.1093/sleep/20.7.505)

6   Rudy, Melissa, "Should you sleep with socks on? Doc reveals the truth about sleeping with warm feet", New York Post (13 October 2023, nypost.com/2023/10/13/doctor-reveals-that-warm-feet-could-be-the-key-to-good-sleep/)

7   Gooley JJ, Chamberlain K, Smith KA, Khalsa SB, Rajaratnam SM, Van Reen E, Zeitzer JM, Czeisler CA, Lockley SW. Exposure to room light before bedtime suppresses melatonin onset and shortens melatonin duration in humans", The Journal of Clinical Endocrinology & Metabolism, vol. 96, issue 3 (March 2011, doi.org/10.1210/jc.2010-2098)

8   Fan, Xiaojun; Liao, Chenxi; Bivolarova, Mariya P; Sekhar, Chandra; Laverge, Jelle; Lan, Li; Mainka, Anna; Akimoto, Mizuho; Wargocki, Pawel, "A field intervention study of the effects of window and door opening on bedroom IAQ, sleep quality, and next-day cognitive performance", Building and Environment, vol. 225 (November 2022, doi.org/10.1016/j.buildenv.2022.109630)

9   EPA.gov, "Care for your air: a guide to indoor air quality", United States Environmental Protection Agency (epa.gov/indoor-air-quality-iaq/care-your-air-guide-indoor-air-quality)

10 Haghayegh, Shahab; Khoshnevis, Sepideh; Smolensky, Michael H; Diller, Kenneth R; Castriotta, Richard J, "Before-bedtime passive body heating by warm shower or bath to improve sleep: A systematic review and meta-analysis", Sleep Medicine Reviews, vol. 46 (August 2019, doi.org/10.1016/j.smrv.2019.04.008)

11 For more replenishing options, seek out the 25 different toolkits in my book *Rest to Reset: The Busy Person's Guide to Pausing with Purpose* (Aster; 2023)

Step 6: Make Meaningful Connections

1   Ong, AD; Uchino, BN; Wethington, E, "Loneliness and Health in Older Adults: A Mini-Review and Synthesis", Gerontology, vol. 62, issue 4 (June 2016, doi.org/10.1159/000441651)

2   Gottman, John M; Levenson, Robert W, "Marital processes predictive of later dissolution: behavior, physiology, and health", Journal of Personality and Social Psychology, 63(2) (August 1992, doi.org/10.1037/0022-3514.63.2.221)

3   Martin, Francois; Bachert, Katherine E; Snow, LeAnn; Tu, Hsiao-Wei; Belahbib, Julien; Lyn, Sandra A, "Depression, anxiety, and happiness in dog owners and potential dog owners during the COVID-19 pandemic in the United States", PLoS One (15 December 2021, doi.org/10.1371/journal.pone.0260676)

4   Grewen, KM; Anderson, BJ; Girdler, SS; Light, KC, "Warm partner contact is related to lower cardiovascular reactivity", Behavioral Medicine, vol. 29 (2003, doi.org/10.1080/08964280309596065)

5   Hertenstein, MJ; Holmes, R; McCullough, M; Keltner, D, "The communication of emotion via touch", Emotion, 9(4) (2009, https://doi.org/10.1037/a0016108)

6   Koole, Sander, "Touch May Alleviate Existential Fears for People With Low Self-Esteem", Association for Psychological Science (psychologicalscience.org/news/releases/touch-may-alleviate-existential-fears-for-people-with-low-self-esteem.html)

7   Murphy, MLM; Janicki-Deverts, D; Cohen, S, "Receiving a hug is associated with the attenuation of negative mood that occurs on days with interpersonal conflict", PLoS One, 13(10) (3 October 2018, doi.org/10.1371/journal.pone.0203522)

8   Monroe, Carolyn M, "The Effects of Therapeutic Touch on Pain", Journal of Holistic Nursing, vol. 27, issue 2 (2009, doi.org/10.1177/0898010108327213)

9   Cohen, S; Janicki-Deverts, D; Turner, RB; Doyle, WJ, "Does hugging provide stress-buffering social support? A study of susceptibility to upper respiratory infection and illness", Psychological Science, vol. 26, issue 2 February 2015, doi.org/10.1177/0956797614559284)

10 Ibid.

11 Inagaki, TK; Eisenberger, NI, "Neural correlates of giving support to a loved one", Psychosomatic Medicine, 74(1) (January 2012, pubmed.ncbi.nlm.nih.gov/22071630/)

12 Ocklenburg, Sebastian, "10 things that make a hug great", Psychology Today (18 June 2022, psychologytoday.com/gb/blog/the-asymmetric-brain/202206/10-things-make-hug-great)

13 Ryan, Richard M, The Oxford Handbook of Self-determination Theory, chapter: "With My Self: Self-Determination Theory as a Framework for Understanding the Role of Solitude in Personal Growth" by Netta Weinstein, Thuy-vy Nguyen, Heather Hansen (OUP USA, 4 April 2023)

14 Masi, CM; Chen, HY; Hawkley, LC; Cacioppo, JT, "A meta-analysis of interventions to reduce loneliness" Personality and Social Psychology Review, vol. 15, issue 3 (August 2011, doi.org/10.1177/1088868310377394)

15 Long, Christopher; Averill, James, "Solitude: An Exploration of Benefits of Being Alone", Journal for the Theory of Social Behaviour, vol. 33 (March 2003, doi.org/10.1111/1468-5914.00204)

16 Abeyta, AA; Routledge, C; Kaslon, S, "Combating Loneliness With Nostalgia: Nostalgic Feelings Attenuate Negative Thoughts and Motivations Associated With Loneliness", Frontiers in Psychology, vol. 11 (23 June 2020, doi.org/10.3389/fpsyg.2020.01219)

Index

Acknowledgements

This book was such a joy to write during the deep dark winter, and as ever, it is a collective accomplishment with many talented people contributing to its creation.

Thank you to my darlings Dave, Charlotte and Teddy, who kindly accompanied me in savouring our local wintry Natural delights. I'll never forget the starlings!

My gratitude goes to Jessica Lacey, my commissioning editor at Aster for trusting me with this theme, and the whole team who made it a seamless and rewarding experience from start to finish – Pauline Bache, my editor, Yasia Williams my art director, and Hazel O'Brien for helping me get the word out.

I had so hoped this book would feel like a warm hug and I thank illustrator Rosanna Tasker for achieving that aim, bringing such light, warmth and colour to the page with her glorious art.

My appreciation also goes to my agent, Jane Graham Maw for being the most impeccable advocate and champion.

Thank you to my community of readers, my clients and my friends on instagram; I love walking the path with you! Thank you for sustaining me with your kind encouragement and sharing with me your winter joy. I hope you enjoy adding some fresh seasonal twists to your self-care toolkits.

About the Author

Suzy Reading is a mother of two, an author, Chartered Psychologist, yoga teacher and coach. Suzy has over two decades of experience in the health and wellbeing industry, working with individuals and organizations in keeping their people happy and healthy. She draws these modalities of psychology, movement and restorative practices uniquely together and is one of the top UK experts on self-care. Suzy is the psychology expert for wellbeing brand Neom Organics and is a founding member of The Nourish App. She figure skated her way through her childhood, growing up on the Northern Beaches of Sydney, and now makes her home in the hills of Hertfordshire, UK.

Also available:

www.suzyreading.co.uk
 @suzyreading